Publishing

Also by Louse Gore Sayer David

John Steel: The Man and the Legend

The *She Heard a Whippoorwill Cry* Series:
Green Sea Plantation
The Land Darkens
Spring's Gift of Light
The Turbulence and the Storm
The Winds Grow Gentle
The Gathering
Half Harvest

The Religious Awakening of Sirus Smith

To Shatter a Cherished Possession

and *Empower Publishing*

The Death of the Neighborhood Church

By

Louise Gore Sayre-David

Empower Publishing
Winston-Salem

Empower

Publishing

Empower Publishing
302 Ricks Drive
Winston-Salem, NC 27103

The book is a work of insight, opinion and experience, and is entirely the product of the author's creative processes. No actual person, place or event is referred to in this work. The author has represented and warranted all ownership and/or legal right to publish all the materials in this book.

Copyright 2024 by Louise Gore Sayre-David

All rights reserved, including the right of reproduction in whole or part in any format.

First Empower Publishing Books edition published
May, 2024
Empower Publishing, Feather Pen, and all production design are trademarks.

For information regarding bulk purchases of this book, digital purchase and special discounts, please contact the publisher at publish.empower.now@gmail.com

Cover design by Pan Morrelli

Manufactured in the United States of America
ISBN 978-1-63066-597-5

For each and all who walked through the door of this church. May we come to know its peace and glory once again.

—Louise Gore Sayre-David

Chapter 1

It set off from the junction of where four dirt rural roads met together and led to four different sections of a community called, Bethel. As likewise to the community it set in, it was known as Bethel Church. And even though it stands no longer, having been torn down and a newer, up-to-date, brick church built in a different location and bearing the same name in the same community, the spirit and warmth within the walls of this old frame church remains to reign in my memory as bright as the light of a newborn day.

It was a square frame building and doubtless not a brick in its construction aside from its foundation, and even its foundation was most likely built of sawed cypress logs. It was painted white, and its appearance was enhanced to some degree by the number of windows on either side of the building that were installed mainly for the purpose of letting fresh air inside. No heating or cooling systems had been heard of in this age in time. In brief, this building had little going for it on the outside to distinguish it from a barn or pack house except its white coat of paint and its steeple erected in the front center of its roof which did indicate that it was a house of worship. The inside enclosed the sanctuary with plain wooden pews on either side of a center aisle that led to an elevated area that consisted of the altar and the pulpit, a section for the choir, as well as a doorway that gave access to two Sunday school rooms walled off from the sanctuary, plus a number of pews to the left of the pulpit, which more often than not was referred to as the amen corner and which was usually occupied by the deacons and leaders of the church. There was no carpet or anything else to mark a degree of elegance, only a plain open interior where one could worship in the manner they chose or were urged to.

However, despite the plainness of this country church or its lack of any enhancement that might have caught one's attention as likewise to the majority of all country churches of that long-ago age, the presence of the neighborhood church was the essential part and symbol that loaned and gave a balance to any and all happenings good or bad that might occur through one's daily life. No other place represented the solace, strength, and reassurance that one strived to seek when overcome with fear and feeling all was lost as this building of worship – the neighborhood church – giving hope and ease to all and any trouble that pained one's heart by entering its doors and feeling the over-riding spirit that ever seemed to prevail within its walls.

Thus, one may think or ask, comparing the fundamental quality that all churches tend to practice today regarding the pattern of the worship service, where has the spirit and passion gone? Certainly, it appears to have become lost and starkly missing in all present-day churches by the changes man has devised and put in motion, laws and rituals and a pattern of worship where the spirit of God's word and His teachings have been replaced by the same mundane religious discourse over and over from one worship service to the next!

There was a time in a long-ago age, and not so many years back in time either, when the neighborhood church was the body or more the soul, so to speak, of the neighborhood as a whole. For not only were those long-ago church services and the social occasions that were connected with the church, as well as all other aspects of life known to us then, seem to have vanished along the way and are no more in favor of a more modern way of going about our daily lives in the present day. No doubt about it, the way of life and our pattern of living that we all adhere to has changed drastically and, in my opinion, this modern change pertains to most all church services of today. The fact is, the church service of today compared to the worship service of those long-ago years hardly holds one spark of the joy and uplifting spirit that those long-ago spiritual occasions generated in one. In truth, and as a rule with hardly any exception, the worship service of today leaves the majority of the churchgoers yearning for the privilege of experiencing the feeling of blessedness and that all is well with the entire world as well as within our own selves when we depart from church and leave for home. Sadly, however, it appears this yearning for the blessedness we seek is not going to be accorded to us no matter how much we yearn and hope for it, if the minister and leaders of the church are not persuaded to take a look back and make an effort to amend the obvious – a lack of spirited belief – and reform the present ritual of how most church services are conducted today and revive the traditional once again.

For instance, one thing among numerous other things that the church would doubtless benefit a great deal from is to revive those old enduring and uplifting hymns of years past, such as, "Love Lifted Me," "My Faith Looks Up to Thee," and "When the Roll is Called Up Yonder," citing only three among so many that are seldom sung anymore. I recall these long-ago hymns being sung in the highest, spiritual homage that man is capable of expressing, sung with such an uplifting spirit and reaching the core of our hearts so deeply by the spiritual wording and soul rending organ music, that one was near brought to tears along with an overpowering urge to see our invisible Savior, Jesus Christ, and possibly touch His person. But, sadly, in the present day we are not granted this spiritual privilege due to man's urge to change the traditional to his way again! Because the hymns that are sung in the majority of churches today are usually selected by the presiding minister, and hymns which he views as being more suitable and appropriate relative to the sermon he has selected for the occasion and which – as a rule – only the choir is familiar with by practice and rehearsal, leaving the congregation most often unable to sing one note, but all the same, most everybody making an attempt to scramble along in hope of finding an element of spirit in the unfamiliar hymn and doubtless feeling nothing aside from their muddle of trying to follow along!

So, by having come by not one degree of inspiration by trying to sing these hymns that, for the most part, we have never heard before, small wonder that a great

The Death of the Neighborhood Church

number of us leave a worship service wondering if we have even gone to church in the first place or merely imagining that we have!

Therefore, regarding the subject of spiritual hymns, it is my view that it would be a good thing to revive these old timeless hymns that were so inspiring and glorified God's teachings so intensely simply because singing induces one to feel good. There is hardly any exception, aside from the singing of hymns in the circumstance of a loved one's funeral, that singing does not inspire a happy and positive outlook even upon feeling that there is little interest or promise of meeting with an urge of enthusiasm that we desire to feel and hold to throughout the day we awaken to.

Certainly, it goes without saying, the minister's sermon is an important part of the church service, too, or it most surely should be, and as enlightening and interesting enough to glorify what Jesus Christ did for mankind. Still, singing old-time spirituals is as much or more to look forward to than any sermon the preacher might select to preach about. In brief, no matter how interesting the preacher's sermon might turn out to be, some old long-time and moving hymn following the sermon is the crowning of the preacher's message and the mark of success regarding the worship service. And yet, it is all about feelings – emotions, the essence of the worship service as a whole. Was it inspiring enough and held enough substance to affect one and stir one's interest to awaken a wandering mind if perhaps there had been a little more noise and explosive blasts from the presiding minister delivering the sermon?

There is no doubt that the majority of ordained

ministers of the present day should give more thought to the above question and consider its importance when they are preparing their own delivery from the pulpit. For in the majority of most sermons we are exposed to in this present day, it seems that most ministers are constantly making an effort to refrain from emphasizing their message with any force whatever in making it clear that there is a heaven as well as a hell regarding the way we conduct our lives! In brief, perhaps worrying and being too concerned about taking a swipe at some, or maybe more than one church member's obvious shady deeds and shortcomings. Which, of course, one can bet that the church member who falls in the shortcoming category is widely known throughout the community and the minister had not polished his or her reputation any at all and should have delivered the sermon in the style it should have been delivered in!

Granted, there is an ongoing decline in church attendance today in all the different denominations of established churches, with maybe an exception here and there of some other religious organizations that are open for divine worship. We might ask ourselves, why is this? What happened to produce this lack of interest in attending church and exposing ourselves to the subject of organized religion? Certainly, something had to intervene that was powerful enough to sway peoples' interest in another direction and turn their minds upon something that engaged and absorbed their attention far more and, to be sure, far more fascinating than any worship service one might be exposed to regardless of how gifted the minister is relative to the style of his delivery!

There is no doubt that the one thing that has played a great part in the decline of church attendance as a whole is the progress that man has made in the field of technology – the invention of a number of startling devices that are at our disposal today and one in particular – television! This powerful and influential device with its classic perfection to bring the ultimate of entertainment into our living rooms by merely pressing on its remote control without our leaving our reclining chairs is truly a wonder to behold. And, what's more, it has the power to hold one's attention fast to whatever its screen is revealing to us no matter one's age – the young and old alike. In addition, nothing is required of us to do but keep our attention glued to this device for as long as we wish, or have the time to give to it, while making ready to attend a church service is a horse of another color! And, needless to say, it is inevitable that the woman of the household is required to put forth far more effort to attend church than what is required of man, even the rare man that does lend a hand from time to time to the normal duties of a household.

First, for the woman of the household, there are always a number of chores that cannot be delayed and put off until she returns from church, mainly the several dishes of food that she has in mind to serve that day and she partially prepares before leaving for church. Then there's the question of what to wear to church, which more often than not, she has thrown two or three different outfits upon the bed before finally making her choice. The next chore is to attack the personal image that she sees staring back at her in the mirror and wondering what in the world to do about her hair, because on this occasion it appears that it is going to require more attention than the lines and wrinkles in her face that, all of a sudden, appear to be more prominent and noticeable as well! All the same, after brushing and combing her hair one way or another and finally deciding no matter how much she attempts to improve the looks of it and sees she is failing in her effort, she lets it fall the way it will and gives a sigh in acceptance and turns to see what she can do about the lines and wrinkles, only to glance at the clock and decides there is little time left to tackle her face if she wants to make it to church on time! So, she reaches for the powder puff and takes one or two swipes with it upon her face and applies a smidgen of rouge – a must because all bloom of youth is long gone – and gives her lips a swipe of lipstick, makes a grab for her purse and car keys, and hoping as she rushes on through the doorway on her way to church that her purse is not too far off in color in matching her shoes! Then on top of all this effort, she starts worrying about her appearance and cluttering her mind by mentally asking herself, will she pass muster, so to speak as well as hoping that with all the effort she has put forth that is surely won't be in vain and she will be gifted with that spiritual uplifting that she is in need of and seeking for herself!

So, considering all these compelling doings above, it should come as no surprise that a great number of people today are choosing to remain in their recliners and press their remote control to a religious sermon on television, rather than venture out to the neighborhood to seek the spiritual inspiration that we all desire and want to feel.

However, in spite of the lure of our recliners and nothing required in the way of what we are wearing from the ordinary as well as making all effort to improve on our physical appearance as a whole, we must concede that when it comes to television versus church, that church should lead in our choice because it does provide us something that television never will, and that is fellowship with our counterparts and the comfort of human contact. In addition, there is a dissimilar mark between the house we dwell in and a house of worship. Whereas being in a house of worship generates a feeling in us of being closer to our divine God and sharing the spirit of His word with others, it will ever be impossible for one to experience this same acclaim with God watching and listening to a worship service on television in our own dwelling no matter how comfortable our recliners feel to us!

Therefore, it should not be asking too much of ourselves to turn our attention back to the church more and give less to television. Surely, we all should be able to spare more restraint away from this seductive invention than we do. Certainly, maybe two hours a week or a little more would not put too much a task on us to give to the church instead of to the ease and comfort of our recliners. Doubtless, the choice would provide us with a better sense of well-being, not only spiritual-wise but a feeling of rightness that we are more in accord with what is just and honorable too.

In possibly everything that man has imagined in his mind and finally brought it to the state of production from the beginning of time, success was solely because he was inspired by an entire spirit to bring it about in the first place, or nothing would have become of his dreams and imagination or anything else he had wanted to achieve. In brief, the core of one's existence is the need to look to a higher power for strength and support to lead and guide them on the road of life – His unseen spirit to encourage them in their disappointments and letdowns to continue on until whatever their hopes and dreams may have been have finally become the reality they were striving for.

There is and has ever been a dormant seed in each and every one of us – whether we will openly acknowledge it or not – to immediately turn beyond man as well as ourselves and call upon God's divine power when we hear grievous news or suddenly meet with some disaster. In nearly every case with hardly any exception, upon hearing shocking news or some horrible happening, the first thought and verbal words we find ourselves expressing is the phrase "Lord have mercy," even though in our shock we are hardly aware we have uttered one word!

To this present day, I recall hearing the sad news from one of my sisters that a brother-in-law, who the entire family held in high esteem, had suddenly passed away with a heart attack. And the first words that I heard myself say to her were, "Lord have mercy" and her response back to me was, "Yes, Lord have mercy." The pain of hearing of his untimely death cuts to the core to this day and remains to be a lingering sadness and sorrow for those who knew him. Doubtless, this staying impact of his death is due to the commendable qualities and makeup of his character as well as the hardship he endured during World Warr II in service to his country, having been forced to parachute from a crashing B-17 bomber in enemy territory and surviving only to be taken a prisoner of war and remain in enemy confinement until the holding prison he was confined in was liberated by American forces in 1945.

All the same, it is a given that none of us escapes loss and grievous experiences in life, and change is inevitable as well and will fall as the years come and go along life's pathway. And yet, although change does fall and more often than not does affect our lives and the customs we are familiar with, and sometimes in more ways than we thought possible and are not prepared for as a rule. However, this different way of meeting life and complying with the unfamiliar should not warrant that the traditional way has no place in our lives anymore and the good we gained from it we need no more. Though the modernized way is usually far more interesting to us and the one we normally embrace and accept. But, even so, why should either be the better choice, modern or traditional?

It is reasonable that an open, profitable and fruitful society needs to welcome and embrace both ways. For there is no question that a society which is not willing to accept and make an attempt to learn the workings of these new and more recent inventions, and remains to cling to the traditional and solely adheres to it alone, would result in a stalemated, standstill society with no progress whatever regarding its development, as well as void of any confidence in man of moving forward and crippling his vision of gaining any future improvement regarding his standard of living.

So, the wonder and miracle are that God did gift man the mind and ability to create and devise the inventions of the past, to say nothing of these incredible new inventions we have at our disposal at the present day, such as television, the cell phone and the computer, which, assuredly, have become prominent fixtures in our lives and which we take a great deal of pleasure and benefit from. And, we should not back away from taking every advantage that these devices offer us. Still, the traditions we followed in the past that we also took much pleasure and delight in, remain to have good and value, too, in our lives, giving us the same joy and uplifting spirit that it did in years past if it were only revived more often than it is. For example, and especially, the one tradition that would generate an overall gladness is if those old, timeless hymns that were sung with such spirit would be sung more often than they are.

Granted, I recall myself singing those age-old hymns so vividly when I was growing up and on into my late teens while attending the neighborhood church on Sunday morning. Those spiritual hymns were a major part of the church service and the one part that seemed to be eagerly awaited by everybody without exception, even those few who happened to be unable to adjust to the musical notes but sang anyway! In that period in time, the singing of those hymns were sung with such a joyful enthusiasm and expectation that it made one feel as though they might have been lifting their voices in some heavenly choir and in the nearness of our unseen God besides, instead of the local church.

And not only did the delight of these moving hymns float inside the church, but the cheerfully rendered singing normally floated beyond the church and gave that uplifting feeling to anyone within earshot also.

But sadly, the above is gone and is no more in this present day. Today, those old moving hymns have nearly vanished from the worship service. More often than not, the hymns that are selected today are hymns that the presiding minister has selected due to his view they are more in parallel and in accord with the topic of the message he desires to convey in his sermon. Of course, only the choir is familiar with it by practicing the minister's selection, leaving the majority of the congregation at a total loss in their effort to follow because, as a rule, they have never heard the hymn before, and finally stop trying to sing it altogether!

In addition, another important factor regarding spiritual hymns, and especially the old enduring hymns, is that they are so moving and uplifting. Rather frequently, when by chance one is selected, no sooner than when the first note of the hymn wafts throughout the church one finds that the tone of the song is nothing like what it was in the past. In the not-too-distant past, I was to experience this additional change from the traditional to the modern when attending church. Having noted that the hymn, "In the Garden," was finally to be a part of the worship service, I was eagerly awaiting to lift my voice to it, only to be sorely disappointed to learn upon the first note of sound from the organ that the hymn had been tampered with. The musical notes were so much different than what I was familiar with that I soon gave up on the new notes that were rendering me no joy whatsoever and remained silent.

Granted, society is benefitted through change and makes for a society that is moving forward. This is good for all people. And yet, changing the notes of these old time-honored hymns is, needless to say, carrying the modern way too far, in my opinion!

Why anyone would be persuaded to change the musical notes of these old long-ago hymns and hear them sung in a different tone from the way they were written and have been sung for untold time is beyond sound reasoning! One wonders, is it the desire to project their own proficiency in the realm of music, a desire to show and display their own capability to create and combine musical notes? If the above question has any foundation, again, it would prompt one to wonder why then they would not have a desire to create something they had devised and written themselves and put their stamp on it rather than fiddle with something someone else has composed and written!

Be that as it may, nothing comes across in the change of things in general any more loud-and-clear than when our national anthem, "The Star-Spangled Banner," is played and sung today. It appears there is no getting around it and no exception to boot, that on any occasion when our national anthem is played to open some celebrated event, that this song is screeched and sung in such a different way by some designated celebrity that one is hard put to even recognize that it is our national anthem, to say nothing of one making an attempt to sing along with music and notes they have never heard before! Though it is assured the living do not know, nor will we ever know, but in this modern fad that "The Star-Spangled Banner" is sung in the present day, it is enough to possibly bring its composer, Francis Scott Key, to turn over in his grave and hide his face in horror as well, so to speak!

It is sad and most regrettable, too, that the late Kate Smith is no longer here to lift her voice to our national anthem in the manner she sang, "God Bless America." For no question, if this were possible, a great number of these noted vocalists of today would be induced to attempt to sing their version of this celebrated song no more, no matter how many opportunities were presented to them, which, of course, would be a blessing bestowed upon everybody!

Chapter 2

If you ask me and doubtless nobody will but hope I am wrong on this, I will make an attempt to express my view about certain things and the way of some circumstances in our society today and truly hope that some will open their ears to it to some degree, because, no question in my opinion, one's ear could come by far worse!

Change. The reader has already heard this word over and over again, or implied relative from the traditional to the modern, and it would be an almost impossible feat to bring one's attention to the whole of this rather long narrative without referring to it time and time again!

To begin with, and there are no two ways about it, when our former President Barak Obama chose the word "Change" to symbolize his campaign for the presidency of this nation – and was successful in his effort to win the election and his right to sit behind that ornate and oversized desk in the White House, as well as the most elevated chair this fair land of America has to offer – he could not have chosen a more appropriate word in his effort to gain the highest office for one to hold in the American process of law had he gone through the dictionary a thousand times or more searching for the right word! But, even so, before I go any further with President Obama's chosen word "Change" to mark his campaign, I feel compelled to

The Death of the Neighborhood Church

point out that whatever high hopes he may have held, if any, to make or improve our society, as a whole, the eight years he was president of this nation it is for certain that it escapes me!

And, it is likewise with the man he was to follow, who occupied the White House for eight years as well, former President George W. Bush! For sixteen long years, I am unable to think of one single law that either of these two presidents devised for the good of this nation and its people and saw that it became law. In truth, to sum up the success of both Obama and George W. Bush's times as Commander in Chief of this nation, it became no better or worse than two teen-age boys playing at shooting a game of marbles while some musical apparatus blared with the recorded notes to the song, "Let the World Go Away"!

Former President Donald J. Trump had the capability as well as the acquired talent to keep this country on an even keel, so to speak, and did, while he occupied the White House. I will stop at making one comment regarding our present President!

However, to President Obama's credit, I must point out that when he chose the word "Change" for the symbol of his campaign to gain the Presidency, it was clearly a coincidence without reason, in that he had not even been born when, in this writer's opinion, the start of the greatest and most shocking change that America has ever awakened to happened on December 7, 1941. The day that Japan made its surprise and sneaking attack on the island of Hawaii, dropping those killing and devastating bombs and taking the lives of well over two thousand souls, as well as nearly obliterating

America's entire naval fleet anchored there in the waters of Pearl Harbor.

Granted, this tragedy at Pearl Harbor, Hawaii, brought untold change and induced the ugly appearance of World War II as well, giving America's sitting President Franklin D. Roosevelt no other choice than asking Congress to declare a state of war against the nation of Japan and its allies, which promptly plunged the United States into a long, four-year war and which was to deeply affect all Americans and their way of life.

Still, at all events, it is inevitable that a state of war is going to bring change and plenty of change at that, change that is combined with so many other facts of life – separation of loved ones and in numerous cases the staying grief of the loss of too many loved ones, sacrifice as well as the deprivation of the necessities of one's daily living pattern, to say nothing of the emotional anxiety of fearing that the way of life and the traditions that we had followed and were accustomed to might vanish for all time like the many lives being lost on the battlefields.

And yet, one continued to hold to hope and faith that the darkness of war would finally end, and the day did appear, thankfully, that we awakened and saw that the sun was still shining without a war clouding its rays and had been shining all along, but the dark of war had prevented us from seeing it.

Of course, wars come and wars go, leaving the loss of lives and the aftermath of ruin and destruction behind, and unfortunately, this has been a given fact since the beginning of creation and time began and will continue to be. As a matter of fact, the Bible speaks of it, Matthew 24:6, stating, there will be wars and rumors of war. Doubtless, this is a part of life and the nature of the make-up of mankind. In brief, it appears to have been a predetermined law from our beginning and destined to be man's fate.

But, even so, we must concede that in the run of things in general, the final say and finding a solution to the problems that arise within the governing of any and all nations lies with the nation's elected officials. And yet, we must acknowledge again, that more often than not, the majority of these elected officials make decisions that have little to do with the good and welfare of the nation and its people, but on how much benefit will come their own way by the stand they take and vote on regarding most any issue of law that confronts them!

One is reminded of the old adage, "it's the nature of the beast." Thus, sadly, it appears that given the opportunity, man will continue to be inclined to put his own interest first and those of whom voted for him to gain office second, if indeed at all!

However, there is and remains one small move that one can make and do in regard to the little that is allowed one to do in any election for a candidate to hold any type of office that controls and enforces the rule of law. Make certain as much as law will allow that you know the make-up, the true beliefs and any or all of the intentions of the candidate you cast a vote for!

In short, again as the saying goes, be careful about the things you pray for, because if your prayer turns out to come your way you could very well be disappointed.

To be sure, the majority of elected officials who hold the seat of government they coveted and finally gained will disappoint us. Too harsh and judgmental? Some in our society would not hesitate to say yes! Then again, giving thought to some of the laws that are being devised and passed by elected officials today in spite of the opposition of a great many Americans, there is no doubt a large number of these same officials would be surprised at the number of people who would answer no, and in capital letters at that! In brief, the status of the election process in the present day has become a dire business, which, of course, induces one to take a look back, and which will sum everything up that is in the making. This nation was founded on the policies that hold to the rules of a democracy, a government in which the power of law is supposed to be held by its people. But, unfortunately, because of these same people electing and voting for inept officials who are not qualified to govern in the first place, it appears this nation is gradually taking on the rule of an autocratic government. In short, instead of a democracy, it is slowly turning to the rule of a dictatorship!

Between the closing of World War I, November 11, 1918, and the beginning of World War II, December 7, 1941, things stayed pretty much on an even keel relative to a great deal of change in our society as well as our customs and our pattern of living. Though there were a number of years in this time period that did continue what came to be marked as the Great Depression when the majority of Americans fell victim to the trials and hardships of trying to survive and hold on in a society that had come to nearly having nothing for one to survive on. In one sense, less the dropping of killing bombs and flying missiles and the shooting of cannons and guns, the state of the economy was hardly any different than had a raging war been taking place. There was great hunger and even starvation in many cases. There were no jobs, paying jobs anyway, because there was no money to pay with. Banks closed. What little money one did have in their possession, they managed it themselves and made every penny go as far as it would to cover whatever happened to be necessary for one's survival. Whatever else remained, one made do with a substitute or did without!

Some people were much better off than others, and especially rural people who owned or resided on farms that exposed them to a great variety of farm foods to eat, unlike the numerous city or town dwellers who were forced to stand in soup lines to keep from succumbing to starvation due to having nothing to eat and no money to buy food with.

Although I was a child and rather young in age during the Great Depression, I hold no memory of being deprived of anything that is required in one's daily living pattern in this period of great strife. No, we were not classified as a rich family. Though I should think we certainly were a privileged family since my father was a planter, and he and my mother owned several hundred acres of land together, and not only seeing to the keep and welfare of their own family, but providing shelter and food for tenants and farm workers as well. In addition, my parents' holdings were within twenty-five, or a little more, miles to the Atlantic Ocean, with its great abundance of seafood of all varieties, which also provided one an enjoyable change in diet fairly often and which my parents saw its benefit and took advantage of.

I recall going to the beach was one of the most pleasurable outings of my childhood, and especially during the first cool, crisp days of autumn when the entire family went to the beach and camped out in a unique place under a canopy of live oaks and hickory trees called Nixon's Grove. We would camp at this place for an entire week. It was a most inviting campground that drew visitors from far and near with numbers of families camping there during the early fall months until the cold of winter began. Several campfires would be glowing each night with people visiting back and forth and becoming acquainted while the womenfolk prepared tasty meals of seafood for their families as the laughter of children playing together resounded and the echoes of joy filled the evening's twilight.

In that day and age, only the cities offered one the comfort of a hotel. The motel had yet to make its appearance. Thus, it was to camp out in the area of the seashore or stay home! Families from as far away as the state of Virginia came to Nixon's Grove to camp and take advantage of the fishing season. As likewise to my own father, the menfolk came not only for the quaint experiences and fellowship that this type of outing provided them, but for the purpose and joy of taking part in pulling the nets of flapping fish from the washing ocean waves so as to have salted fish to eat for long weeks after returning home. There was no scarcity of fish in those days. When a school of fish was spied near the shore by some man who was stationed on lookout, he gave a signal for the fishermen to take the longboat out and drop the fish nets behind the school of fish, which the fishermen wasted not one second in doing, and within minutes they and their counterparts were grabbing a hold on the loaded nets of fish and pulling their bounty from the washing surf. It was some awesome sight to see thousands upon thousands of fish flailing and flapping in the nets. One could purchase the fish for nearly nothing, and sometimes the catch was so leavy the fish were given away.

Aside from the crude fishing shacks where the fishermen housed their longboats and fishing nets, maybe in distances every mile or more from the other, the entire coastline was a barren natural environment, free of any clutter save what nature had built and erected over the centuries. For instance, as far as the eye could see the beaches were lined with snow white sandbanks from the ocean tides washing in and out in a continuous motion in untold time, to say nothing of the added hurricanes with their raging force of winds and tides that had been a great help in building these sandbanks, with a number of them reaching the height of a two-story building. There was not a weed, bush or tree anyplace, nothing but this innate and astounding wonder that make a unique and excellent playground for children, which my twin brother and myself took advantage of every chance that came our way. We would climb to the top of the tallest sandbank we could find and then lay flat on the sand and roll over and over to the bottom! I can now hardly imagine us engaging in this form of play for hour upon hour without breaking a limb once!

In addition to playing on the sandbanks, there was also the wading and frolicking in the breaking and washing ocean waves on the shore as well as the delightful and interesting pastime in searching and looking upon the millions and millions of beautiful seashells of all colors, sizes and shapes that the ocean tides had deposited on shore in a continuous rhythm by time.

Today, the coastal beaches are totally void of how they were in long years back, when for the most part, the entire coast looked as though not one footstep of man had touched it since God had had His hand upon it in the time of His creating the universe. Moreover, it seemed back in that age in time, a universal feeling of all people was more in harmony not only with God's creation and the wonder of all the things He made for us to look upon and enjoy, but the promise of His nearness was more profound and deep within one's being as well. And, this spiritual awareness seemed to be more steadfast and real during the church revivals and the occasion of the hymnal conventions, as well as the church anniversaries, all of which were held fairly often and which the entire surrounding neighborhoods looked forward to and happily engaged in.

To be sure, the church revivals of those bygone days were very much unlike the church revivals of the present day, which have been cut down to the usual two nights of worship service – maybe three nights with Sunday night worship service – and which hardly qualifies to be called a church revival!

The church revivals back in time began on a Sunday

night following the Sunday morning worship service of the chosen week for the revival meetings that were held each evening throughout the entire week. Further, the baptismal rites following the weekly revivals were another spiritual event to take place and look forward to, and especially relative to the Baptist church that requires a Believer to be immersed in water. Thus, since there was no inside pool facility in those days, it was not uncommon to see long lines of people gathered at some shallow place on a nearby riverbank waiting to be baptized following a Baptist revival! Of course, although the Methodist church baptism was no less spiritual and moving, it nevertheless was far simpler with only sprinkling of water from a font required. All in all, there is hardly any comparison between those church revivals back in time to the two-day church revival that is the custom in the present day, unfortunately.

The occasion of the hymnal sings referred to as a singing convention was another joyful and delightful experience. The church choirs from a number of churches gathered together at one particular church to lift their voices in song in a single choir together, which of course, with this large assembly of organized singers all lifting their voices in spiritual hymns together was another most unique and uplifting custom that everybody enjoyed and held in great expectation.

Sadly, however, this spiritual custom of old that did induce a feeling of cheer and gladness in one no matter how low the spirit has totally been done away with, and nothing of spiritual worth replacing it besides! Nowadays, one feels lucky upon taking a look at the worship program if they observe that one of the old familiar hymns is finally going to be a part of the service for once. For, as a rule today, the presiding minister of the church mostly selects the hymns that he feels are related and more in accord with the sermon he has prepared and will give more substance to his delivery of it. Actually, in truth, the hymns are a major part, or maybe the most important part of a worship service. For, in this writer's opinion, no matter how gifted a minister is in devising his sermon and his delivery of it, he is unable to match the wording or the inspiration that the old familiar hymns induce in one to hear in song. Because, in brief, singing simply makes one feel good, and especially singing those old enduring hymns such as, "My Faith Looks Up to Thee," "The Old Rugged Cross," "Amazing Grace," and "Love Lifted Me" four among so many we seldom hear anymore, or maybe once or twice a year, if then!

To culminate some of the church customs of years past, the annual anniversary celebration appeared to take priority over all the other church celebrations as well as all the other social gatherings connected with the church. There was no special date set aside for the event to take place since it usually occurred on the date a church was established, or near the date some record might reveal the church was built, because in some cases there was no record only by word of mouth. However, despite the question of the exact date, the church anniversaries usually took place in late spring when the yearly crops were all in the ground and beginning in their growth, or in the Indian summer days of autumn when the crop year was either finished, especially the tobacco crop, or ebbing to the final stage of production as with the sweet potato crop.

The anniversary event was an entire day of socializing and fellowship with one's neighbors, friends and acquaintances. It was a day filled with a worship service in the morning as well as in the afternoon, to say nothing of the joyful singing of the uplifting hymns and the unique adventures of eating a savory and delectable dinner spread out on a white tablecloth upon the church grounds. In the case of rainy weather, the church pews served as a place to spread the picnic style dinner. In this period of time, there was no recreational facility, only the church for worship service and the necessary outhouse. Some churches did have a sunken water pump with a pump handle to pump fresh water from some underground water source. Some churches had no source of water, not even an open well dug several feet into the ground. These open wells were enclosed at ground level with wooden boards or brick and displayed a four-sided frame of support above the well with a bucket attached to a chain to draw the water from below to the surface. Of course, the church that had no well or water pump, one's water or other beverage was brought from home.

The annual church celebration did require more in preparing to attend it than any of the other church events. But in spite of all the preparation required to attend, or take some part in its program, it appeared the entire countryside looked forward to the occasion and truly took much delight in doing all that was required of one to be present for it!

First, there was one's clothing attire to consider and

get together for the occasion. Actually, as a rule, a total new outfit was either bought already made or one assembled it on their own. Of course, a new outfit was certainly not required or expected, and even though this was the case, everybody without exception desired to appear looking as presentable and up-to-date as they possible could. My mother was a gifted seamstress. I recall she sat at her sewing machine hour upon hour making beautiful outfits for my sisters and me to wear to this special event. The dresses she made for us would have done credit to the costliest store-bought dress anyplace, displaying far more than merely plain sewing a dress pattern together. Our dresses were embellished with all different kinds of needlework, lace trimming, braid, embroidery, ornamental buttons and beads, as well as beautiful ruffles added from the same type of material the dress was made of. Of course, the material for the dresses was seasonable and depended on the time of year the church anniversary was to take place – light and airy material such as voile and crepe for spring and summer, and a heavier and darker material for autumn and the winter months.

In addition to the clothing issue, there was the task and question of the different dishes of food to consider and be readied to take to church on the day of the anniversary event. With no refrigerator in this time period available to the average family, any types of food that required to be kept at a cold temperature, such as cold salads and other fancy fixings, were out of the question. Still, despite the cold, icy fixings having no place in this unique adventure of eating far from the comfort of the dining room, there were all kinds of other delectable dishes of eats at one's disposal.

And even though the question of refrigeration was a problem in this time period, and especially if one did not dwell in a city or town, most families did have an icebox to store ice in. And the question of keeping food cold or having icy fixings to eat was solved by buying ice by the block at a place of business in the nearest city or town called an icehouse. The icebox was sufficient for storing a block of ice, or one could purchase the ice by any pound they desired to have.

All the same, the anniversary event was a most enjoyable occasion for everybody. Families, as well as neighbors, had an opportunity to visit back and forth in fellowship and catch up on all the local happenings of late, not to mention, engage in a smidgen of gossip and come by a rumor or two to boot! Children ran and played together with glee, while the teenagers looked and gazed at one another in all their innocence and often as not found their gaze locked to the other in mutual attraction, which in a great number of cases resulted in courtship and, eventually, marriage. Courtship in those years between a young man and a young woman was far more unworldly and an innocent affair than it is in the present day. There was no telephone service in the rural areas until the post-war years following World War II. Only a city or nearby town had telephone service. So, writing a letter and hoping it would reach the address of the girl he had in mind and into her hand informing her of his desire to call on her on a certain date, nothing else was left to do but for him to take a chance and venture on out on his mission and hope for the best! Moreover, paying court to the opposite sex was seldom done aside from Saturday night and Sunday afternoon. And if the occasion was merely a chance mission the young man was on, he was well aware that he may be exposing his intentions and himself to other suitors who might have already arrived before he made his appearance. If this turned out to be the circumstances, all concerned made the best of the situation and handled it with dignity. There were no fistfights even if a number of the young men felt the urge to smack one another for it was an unspoken law that bending to this type of behavior, the young woman involved would have been off limits to each of them for all time!

A Sunday afternoon outing for a young couple to be together was the general rule. And yet, when the sun began to sink on the western horizon, it was manifest the couple begin to make tracks for the girl's home in order to arrive back before dark! No courting was allowed outside the home after dark. If it happened to be a cloudy day with no sun to signify that daylight was falling, most young men made sure they had some kind of timepiece on themselves! To a great degree, this custom to be home before dark was most absurd, if not ridiculous, because engaging in naughty behavior is certainly not limited to the dark of night if one is so inclined to do so!

Still, for the most part, those past days were a chaste society with only a reputation falling from grace every now and then. To be sure, it was a far cry from what it is today. In truth, there is hardly any measure of parallel between then and the present day, which as astonishing as it is, one may witness a bride dressed in virgin white from head to toe and no more than a week away from giving birth to the baby she is carrying, moving toward a flower bedecked altar toward her groom to exchange their marriage vows!

Furthermore, the scene appears to be as much acceptable as if she were slim as a reed and truly as virgin as any bride who has ever approached a church altar to be married!

Today, to quote the song, "Anything Goes," and no one is surprised in the least no matter how far off the beaten track the scene has come from the normal. As likewise to the decline in church attendance, given the fact that moral behavior has nearly become lost in today's society, no one person should become too surprised or maybe moved to ask, what happened? For with the value of moral behavior having become so unlimited, there is little wonder left, let alone to justify the majority of accepted customs of the present day!

However, speaking of chaste standards, in the days of the yesteryear, with morals being as they were, it was nearly impossible for a courting couple to see beyond one's personal appearance or what little each was willing to reveal in some particular circumstance. Because, more often than not, a high number of couples were hardly more than strangers upon marriage, and certainly the physical side of their nature remained to be a mystery to both until they were ensconced in their marriage bed! So, considering how little they both were familiar with the likes and dislikes about the other, in some cases, it probably took a lifetime for some couples to truly feel that they had finally become acquainted with one another!

Furthermore, this type of relationship between a couple and especially with the shy and introverted doubtless had its worth in that it generated many appealing surprises as well as an element of continuing anticipation that kept a great deal of dullness away from a husband-and-wife relationship, which may have accounted for so few couples divorcing one another and which was so seldom heard of in those long-ago days.

All the same, despite the vast measure between moral decline in the present day compared with the chaste custom of bygone days, the divorce rate has grown and has come to be far more prevalent and nearly about as common as the institution of marriage. Hence, it is safe to conclude that the loose morals of today with unmarried couples living together under the same roof and in some cases, having children together without the sanctity of pledging their love for one another in wedded matrimony – to say nothing of same sex couples – that no one person who is involved is being rewarded not one degree relative to having any solid security whatever, to say nothing of all healthy aspects for success are hindered for said couples living under these types of arrangements.

Moreover, this custom of open behavior today, brides decked out in virgin white from head-to-toe with a flowing veil fluttering around her person as well as obviously on the verge of being rushed to the delivery room with the baby she is carrying before she reaches the altar to exchange marriage vows with her bridegroom, same sex couples desiring to seal their relationship in a legal marriage, not to mention some couple whom have already lived together for long years

The Death of the Neighborhood Church

and in the majority of cases having a number of children together suddenly up and decides to stage a formal wedding to one another with all the fanfare and flourish that this kind of social event calls for! But, even so, scarcely one word of surprise or one word of dissent will one hear relative to such outlandish doings. In brief, all the above circumstances are accepted as the norm today with very few attendants, if any, seeing anything out of the ordinary with these absurd and incredible events!

Of course, all these doings in our present-day society are ridiculous, and especially if we consider that we are long centuries from the doings of the ancient caveman and should be more cultured than to adhere and accept these uncommon doings. For our society in the present day is a far cry from that of ancient days, because centuries of civilization consisting of order and refinement have been put at our disposal, whereupon the caveman dwelled in a primitive state of existence with no ordered lifestyle or civilized culture at his disposal. Nor were there any rules of order for him to copy or follow. He was forced to live by instinct alone with no pattern of decorum to guide him relative to his conduct and behavior.

So, considering some of the absurd and unreasonable goings-on in our present-day life, one is induced to wonder with all the progress and advantages we have come by, why it appears we seem to be nearly reverting back to a custom of living that is hardly not too far off from the beaten track of those ancient dwellers who were innocents in their lifestyle, which of course, we are unable to claim and which we certainly are not entitled to have an excuse whatsoever for all the loose moral practices we are seeing today as well as to the extent our standard of living has been transformed to.

Thus, no doubt about it, it appears that free expression is the vogue to follow nowadays in every aspect of our living pattern. And, to make matters worse, it is obvious that some of the laws that are devised and required to be ruled on – from city council to the Supreme Court – the final say on any rule of law – that the majority of our elected officials are incapable of interpreting or giving sound thought to the lasting harm and deterioration that these said laws will, eventually, bring to the populace of any society in the long run and possibly wounding it so badly that any chance of it even healing will be nearly impossible!

Granted, it seems that in this present day the mode is not only free expression of oneself, but to do so it is assumed will make one more stable and adjustable to the consequences of life, to say nothing of preserve one from self-serving as well as self-indulgent tendencies, and is the approved and better pattern for one to follow!

Be that as it may, however, despite the decline in the convention of marriage, the breakdown in our society as a whole, as well as the established rules of law, it appears the majority of our elected officials and the greater number of the populace and a large number of ordained ministers, too, all back away from viewing this obvious break-up in our society as being offensive whatsoever or make one move to repel it anyway at all!

In brief, it is a given summation that no society will continue to endure with an ongoing decay in all aspects of its broken form. Certainly, without reversing this current deterioration that is in progress before it becomes worse, it will continue to grow and, eventually, destroy all that is decent and morally right in holding a society together until it finally falls altogether and nothing will be left to mend!

Because of its continuing to glorify its sinking degeneration and its morals, ancient Rome fell and became extinct, lost to history forever. Hence, we all should take heed of Rome's downfall regarding our own society as well as keep in mind that God is not pleased with all these unpleasant doings and happenings that are taking place among us today. Therefore, it is essential that each and all begin to give more serious thought to this matter of free expression in every manner of lifestyle in the present day, to say nothing of the question of its consequence on a people as a whole. Reflecting more on the subject, it appears the disclosure of one's sexual orientation – their preference for one thing over another regarding this private and personal side of life is the accepted rule and most popular move to follow nowadays, which is beyond the power of reason for one to understand!

Pray tell me, why should anyone care to know or be interested in this side of another person's behavior or choice, that is, aside from those who do share physical contact or a deep personal closeness with another? Certainly, it is unreasonable to view that this type of disclosure is necessary for the entire populace to know!

One must think or ask, will making known the private side of anyone's personal life formulate a more honorable, honest and efficient person in the workplace, or a more appealing and suitable one in every walk of life from the highest office in the land to the running of a household? I should think not!

But, even so, and unfortunately, this open, free expression appears to be the current and approved style to follow in this present day. And yet, perhaps one reason for its appeal, doubtless one among many, is the highest elected official in our society for example calling some noted celebrity on the phone and congratulating them for disclosing their sexual preference to the entire nation! Thereby, there is little room left to wonder that the ethics of the country is rapidly falling into decline despite the numerous citizens whom are saddened and greatly disapprove of the state of affairs of this nature as well as the standards of our society as a whole.

Chapter 3

Since time beginning of God's Creation of the universe and the whole body of things that made it what it is, man has endured because of these things as well as faith and hope and, yes, wonder too, that He made available to us to use and enjoy. The land, the seas, the air, the sky, the moon and the stars in the heavens above us, which He created and which is ever there and more visible to the eye in the dark of night – a heavenly beacon that He put there for the benefit of man to not only take delight in the unique beauty and wonder of both shining light upon a dark world, but a permanent signal for the lost to find direction in their steps again and, pointedly, regarding the gleaming stars above.

Granted, God created and gave all the above wonder to man to enjoy and take benefit from out of His love for us. And yet, as one may marvel over these unique and wonderful gifts He gave to us, we might also ask ourselves have we thanked God and appreciated and used them in the manner He trusted us with and be pleased with. This is a question for all people to ponder and reflect upon. In truth, taking into account how man has and is ill-treating some of these earthly resources, it is doubtful that He is pleased.

From what history tells us about the way of life and the manner in which the native Indians viewed the earth and all the rest of its natural wonders in back centuries, man in this present day would do well to stop and consider the vast difference and, in some respect and degree, heed this obvious disparity between then and now and before it is too late to alter it. It appears that in the antiquity of earth and man that there was an ingrained instinct in the latter to recognize in this great age that earth and its natural wonders were to be protected and a given to hold in reverence – for the most part – instead of being taken for granted and would remain intact for man to use as he sees fit to do for all time to come regardless of all the abuse heaped upon them.

Something else to give thought to and possibly ask ourselves, where has that great quantity of faith and hope that were so abundantly held back in the ages gone to? No better example to fall back on will we find in a people than those who boarded the Mayflower, a wooden and defective sailing ship that had seen its better days, to brave an over three thousand miles of unknown ocean for the purpose of feeling free to worship God in the manner and way they desired to. Yes, the Pilgrims who founded Plymouth colony in the year 1620 were this type of people united in a common bond and interest, a people so endowed with a deep faith and abiding belief in God and His teachings that they had no qualms to set their vision westward and seek the goal of their faith. One is moved to contemplate if this class of people who were united together in a common cause of faith and unity, a faith so deeply imbedded within them that it gave them the courage to seek an obscure undertaking and a hope as well that the purpose they sought would be gained, could be found in the present-day society? Sadly, it is doubtful.

It seems that this all-out characteristic of faith and hope and promise for better things to come that propelled one forward into the unknown centuries ago have gradually become less and less obvious in this day and age, having been replaced by too many people who only display self-seeking traits and interests that concern themselves and no one else. We see and hear so much of this self-interest today. And yet not too many years back, I, myself, can recall that this self-absorption was not the pattern or custom among people and, certainly not among neighbors as well as for the most part the general public as a whole.

No question, however, about all the changes that have taken place and are practiced, we are fortunate that it has taken decades upon decades to bring these changes and habits in one's moral character about. As a matter of fact, a large number of accepted customs today were unheard of only a few decades back. In addition, any shocking or unusual behavior would not have been tolerated any longer than the time it had taken for it to occur and that would have been the end of it! Granted, it would not have become a conversational subject for the populace to hold their view on and have their say, not to mention the local newscast if not the national news and the police department as well! For the most part, those trivial and inconsiderable occurrences back in the past decades were handled as a rule by some older person, or maybe one or two others in the community who were respected for their obvious knowledge and leadership. Then the matter was laid aside and, if not totally forgotten about, it certainly did not become something to occur over and over again and the shock of it become a near accepted act of behavior as being the norm as it is today!

Indeed, one may give thought to it and ask themselves, what brought all this crazy and unheard of behavior into our way of living in this present day? Is it because of all the technology, not to mention the advancement at our disposal not only in the workplace but in our daily lives as well? Doubtless the contrast between yesteryear and this day and age has had a deep impact. For those earlier settlers who were very much aware of their struggle for survival in a harsh and strange land, and under primitive conditions at that, were not going to come about because of their strength alone, no matter their determination. Thus, man in this earlier age appears to not only have had a closer affinity and harmony with others, and especially his neighbors, but it also appears there was an ever-staying element of feeling closer in spirit with God as well.

Granted, that building in every neighborhood with its steeple pointing above to the heavens seemed to be the symbol of strength and the place that only could give one the comfort they yearned for and needed when every so often, and unexpected at that, that trouble of some kind as well as despair and pain of spirit nearly overwhelmed them. And yet, there was that ever shelter of refuge to seek and the symbol of one's hope, the neighborhood church. Merely walking through its doorway and on into its sanctuary induced one to feel that no matter how bleak the outlook of things seemed to be that all would turn for the better. Yes, indisputably, that everlasting spirit of God, which is

The Death of the Neighborhood Church

always there and which never fails to ease our hearts and wounds upon turning to Him and in His house of worship. But, even so, and as depressing as it is to acknowledge this deep spiritual feeling that the mere sight of the neighborhood church generated in the majority of people in past decades has declined and ebbed so obviously in our daily lives that passing by the neighborhood church nowadays has no more an impact, and especially spiritual, than passing by some other building! Further, and sadly at that, the attendance in all churches, if not already rapidly declining is following in the same order as the spiritual decline that the church building itself is undergoing!

Questions upon questions abound, one wonders and is moved to ask, what has caused so many pronounced changes in our daily lives today? And more to reflect upon is the pace of life in this present day. It seems there is forever an undercurrent urging one to hurry no matter the mission we are set upon, or the deed before us that is to be completed. It seems there is an inner clock in all of us constantly ticking the minutes away and persuading us to feel that we must hurry to get the task done, or the errand we set out to run over with as quickly as we possibly can. And, what's more, the pace appears to be increasing as surely as the clock continues to tick the time away. It has become very nearly like some newscast has announced that time is on its way out and we must speed forth and take advantage of its duration while it is in existence!

One may ponder as well as wonder if all the new inventions and technology that we have at our disposal today have produced this urge within us to hurry so? Is it the fascination that some of these products give us that prompts one to turn to them every opportunity that comes our way instead of taking a moment or two to stop and "smell the roses", so to speak, not to mention taking delight in the smell as in a former time!

However, despite our apparent and compelling need to rush through any given day in our lives as well as the distraction we meet with because of all the inventions and technology, these products have greatly been a blessing to man and improved his workday in many forms and especially aided his own physical strength in untold ways.

For instance, giving credit to a mere few that have greatly assisted man – and woman too – in their daily tasks and much improved it in the manner it was done, such as the iron plow and later the farm tractor, the cotton gin, the sewing machine, which has saved woman hour upon hour from sewing clothes and making numerous other things with a mere sewing needle! Relieving man from using his ultimate physical strength in many circumstances regarding the task facing him, to say nothing of the brute force that was required for decades upon decades from those four-legged creatures of the animal kingdom. The oxen and the mules and the horses used in clearing the land and turning it into fertile soil. The early settlers – man and woman too – guiding these work animals into a westward, uncharted land as they pulled the overloaded wagons from daylight until the dark of night, not to mention holding onto the reins of these work animals until their hands became numb from the strain of it. Further, the teamsters who also hauled all types of goods, handmade as well as manufactured, in the business of transportation, which of course, required the guiding of these work animals as well. Then, thankfully, the motorized engine was invented, relieving man as well as those beasts of burden in more ways than one could hardly count or imagine!

Granted, the farm tractor was a godsend to both man and those beasts of burden when it came to tilling the land. It is unbelievable the progress that has been made in farming the land. It has come to be no rare occurrence to see a farm tractor with an enclosed canopy attached to it, protecting its operator from untold misery of all kinds of brutal weather conditions from rain to sleet storms and summer heat that sometimes reaches to the one-hundred-degree mark or maybe above that. And going back to the cotton gin that saved both man and woman many hours of hard work picking the seed from a cotton boll with their fingers, which most often caused the worker to endure a lot of pain and aching in their fingers and hands. And, in addition, relative to the womenfolk and the sewing machine, next came the miracle of the zipper and sliced bread as well! So many numerous inventions that have improved living conditions in general for all people as well as changing working conditions in all types of labor that have benefitted each and all in our society.

Still, the question is and I fear will remain a lasting question, what will be the final impact that some of these newer technical inventions and devices have on our society as a whole? Namely, the cell phone comes to this writer's mind! Since this technical invention has made its appearance into our lives, I often find myself questioning its value against its possible liability to society because of the obvious impact it has made on all ages – young and old alike. Though our way of communicating by regular landline phone is certainly satisfactory and equal in service and probably more beneficial and safer to us in general than the cell phone, this captivating device has charmed its use into all walks of life and by the majority of people to boot as well as all ages from even babies old enough to grip onto it to parents, grandparents and even in the case of great-grandparents!

To be sure, it seems there is no escape from the cell phone no matter the circumstance or type of the occasion. It truly is amazing to witness its power of distraction and absorption and the seeming grip it holds on its user from the entertainment of rock and roll, a worship service in church, or even the somber rites of a funeral!

It is not unusual to see someone turn to their cell phone to make contact, or see the image of the person they have an urge to see, even while the minister is delivering his sermon. It appears no matter the occasion, or how important or how solemn the event, the cell phone comes to be a part of it before it is over. It is no surprise or unusual sight to see three and four-year-old children with a cell phone clapped to their ears. In addition, it is a common practice, and a dangerous one at that, to see numerous people driving their cars at a high rate of speed on a highly busy interstate highway with a cell phone clapped solidly to their ear carrying on a conversation as though they were sitting in their recliner at home, which, of course, the law should put a stop to!

Little wonder the urge to seek the company of a neighbor in person and enjoy a conversation, or anyone else for that matter, when the cell phone is so handy to reach for.

Be that as it may, however, the cell phone is here and, doubtless will remain in our lives and become no less a permanent fixture to turn to as looking at a timepiece to see what time it is.

So be it!

Chapter 4

Change. The word alone is composed of so many components that it is impossible to take in its power of producing so many elements that make up our lives as well as generating the energy of turning our minds in an altogether different course or direction than what we would have dreamed or foreseen, not to mention the impact it brings to our way of living, which as a rule has no similarity whatever to our former living pattern.

And, the pattern of change not only applies to the cell phone, but also to the numerous other technical devices that have been invented and now hold so great a part of our attention and interest that, sadly, there appears to hardly be enough space left in our minds to give thought beyond these devices that have nearly come to stopping us from using our own ability to discover other interests in life as well as solving, or attempting to find a solution to a problem ourselves.

There are so many other facets that make up our living pattern and give thought to and focus our minds on, and especially our God, and His house of worship, who bestowed our life to us and all other things that make up our daily living, in the first place. Still, in truth, it appears our awareness of God and His teachings and blessings are gradually diminishing and being replaced by our own interests and our absorption with these technical devices that are so numerous today.

To be sure, all the above is not to imply that the cell phone and all other technical devices that have come into our lives and changed our normal way of doing things is not to our good and beneficial to us in more ways than we could have imagined. And yet, to become so absorbed and fascinated with the workings and startling function of these devices that we allow them to take over our minds from our awareness of some situation or circumstance we may find ourselves in is totally out of reason. In brief, it is ridiculous to witness a grownup reach for their cell phone like some child fascinated with a new toy no matter the occasion or event.

Granted, the cell phone as likewise to all other inventions that have been introduced to us and are a part of our lives have, for the most part, made all labor easier for us to do as well as better and more beneficial to us in numerous ways. And yet, we should be wiser and realistic in the way we view the matter. For as it is with all things we encounter in life, whether personal or otherwise, all that is relevant has its place! Therefore, to allow our minds to become so absorbed by these technical devices there is also the possibility at the same time that we are hindering our own talents and capability from achieving any growth or success on its own. In brief, there is a big chance of our shortchanging ourselves. Still, it is most persuasive to turn to these inventions and let them do our mental work for us rather than make the effort to do whatever needs to be done ourselves!

Thus, the question will continue to hang and should concern all of us. What effect will all this technology, as well as all the astonishing and awesome technical methods that are so widely popular today, have on the younger generation, and especially children in the classroom who are exposed from first grade throughout their school years to the computer? This wonder invention that seems to hold the key to any and all things that one seeks to know or find the answer to. Hence, the only thing left hanging in the balance is to discover its key!

At all events, one is moved to ponder and truly question what did cause so much change to occur in our lives and turn our pattern of living and our way of doing things totally around from previous years back? Doubtless, the answer does point to all this new technology and our habitual use of it has induced the difference, or would our habits and customs have made a turnabout in any case? It is rational to conclude that despite these astonishing devices or anything else that might have shown up to our disposal that change would have fallen anyway, because it is inevitable and a part of life and has ever been from time beginning.

All the same, and even though all parts of society are affected by change, it appears the institution of the church has certainly not been spared. Indeed, if the present-day attendance of all churches tells us anything, this established custom of worship has been greatly affected, no matter the denomination of the church.

Indeed, it has not been so far back in time when the pews of all churches, and especially the local neighborhood church, were filled with churchgoers from end to end on any given Sunday as well as when other social events were held in the church. Another uplifting factor was the cheerful look of expectation glowing on the face of most everyone in attendance, a feeling of high enthusiasm that only being in the church inspired one to feel. In fact, it was not an unusual occurrence for no space to be left on the church pews, and additional chairs were placed in the church corridor to accommodate those standing. But regretfully, it has come to be a different story today with the majority of all churches. Those same church pews that used to be occupied in full by all those churchgoers with their eager-looking faces will have no more than maybe three or four people occupying an entire pew, and some pews will be totally empty!

One is persuaded to give serious thought to why so many in society have lost so much interest in attending church in this present day. Is it because we have so many material things to attract our attention today that were unavailable to us in the not-too-distant past? Granted, a great deal of the lost interest in attending church can be traced to some of these technical devices, which, for the most part, are geared to produce so many amazing and astounding distractions and so masterfully at that, that our interest in attending church as well as our habits in general are pushed to the side to await to be done, having become far less important to us than they might have once been. But, even so, we might stop and take time to consider our obvious fascination with all these technical devices and wonder if we are losing all perspective to whatever that was once important to us. All those things that we once viewed as being of value and worthwhile to our daily living could slowly begin to become less and less meaningful to us and gradually fade into obscurity until the significance of the impact those things made on our lives is lost to us forever with no chance of ever reviving it no matter how intense the desire within us to see, live and experience this way of life again.

And yet, despite the appearance of all the technology and technical devices that are at our disposal and have made such a deep impact on our lives, as well as changed our custom and way of living so greatly, and most importantly, church attendance, man, himself, is responsible for a great deal of it because of his lack of discipline to hold to his normal routine of attending church.

In addition, the majority of ministers as well should bear the brunt also for their own ineptness in the manner in which they deliver God's word and His teachings, to say nothing of their nonchalant attitude regarding their position as the leader of the church they are serving! Though it is fact there is not one minister serving in any denomination who would view himself as falling into an inept category of any type, and especially those who hold a Ph.D. in Theology! But, even so, one must acknowledge that the ministry is no different from any other profession when it comes to the question of one being capable or suited to the profession they have chosen as their life's work. The question remains, that in spite of any sphere of degree one may hold relative to the vocation they have chosen to follow, do they have the talent and the proficiency to do justice and carry through with the duty that some matter they are confronted with requires of them? To be sure, some do, some do not!

For instance, regarding the summation above. Granted, some church ministers are endowed with the calling to serve Christ, possessing the talent to deliver God's word and His teachings as well as the ability to persuade others to seek the gift of God's love and serve Him, not to mention, love their fellow man also and help him as near within their own means as possible. However, and unfortunately at that, there are many ordained ministers who for certain would have been wiser and served society far better if they had chosen some other profession!

In short, not only do a great number of ordained ministers today fall way short in having the ability to bring people closer in harmony with God and one's fellow man, but also fail in building up the attendance of the church they are serving as its minister none whatsoever!

Further, the churches in this present day, and it appears there is no exception regardless of the denomination, have become too involved in other interests and social work and doings, and in a number of cases letting those things take priority over the teachings of God's word and all the other interesting and numerous things the Bible tells us as a whole. Actually, some churches in this day and age function more on the order of a social club rather than a house of God! Though back in an earlier time the custom of paying respect to God was vastly different. Thus, the question left to ponder is, have all the social doings in the churches at present along with technology shifted peoples' minds away from what a house of God stands for and represents whether they are inside its walls or not affected their desire to attend church in the first place?

And yet, another something could play a part and be a reason for less interest in attending church in person. Seldom is there a church program printed today without some notice inserted along with the program asking for a contribution of some sort, and more often than not, is to be sent to some order or group of people in a foreign country at that! Granted, it is good to hold an open heart. But it is also good and far more reasonable to let charity and goodwill be distributed to the needy and unfortunate in one's own community and country at home, and let those foreign countries take care of their own. Certainly, this statement sounds cold-hearted and totally indifferent. However, it is also reasonable and safe to assert that the larger part of these foreign contributions, if not all, that are sent to aid the needy goes into the pockets of the officials involved instead! For such is the love of money! So, why not keep the underprivileged in mind in one's own community or country and do what we can to help them?

All the same, and speaking of money, it goes without saying and should not be questioned one degree, the two most important life's work that one may choose to serve society, as well as earn a living, are the clergy and the study of medicine. For no other vocations bring people in closer contact with one another, emotionally, spiritually, and physically. Therefore, those who have in mind to seek either of these two professions should give a great deal of thought and consideration to all that will be required of them once they are adapting to or practicing their career. Are they themselves emotionally and physically able to take on someone else's health problems, not to mention the question of life itself in the case of a physician, and do justice to the patient or person involved in either case health-wise or spiritually?

At all events, in respect to some church ministers who may have chosen the wrong profession in regard to building up the attendance at his or her church that they have been assigned to, much less have the ability to persuade their congregation to seek a closer relationship with God and obtain salvation, they are not alone and have plenty of company among the medical physicians today!

Indeed, the number is great among the medical doctors today who should have sought another career! For when it comes to having any bedside manner whatsoever, there are numerous doctors treating the ill who are simply incapable of communicating with the patient they are administering to, not to mention falling way short in recognizing the symptoms of the indisposed and prescribing the necessary medication!

In brief, perhaps society would have been far better off and benefitted to the good in general far more had a number of doctors of today chosen to have worked in a department store. For finding the style, color and size of a shoe that someone else has already selected and taking it to them requires little brain work, and one can chuck the personality!

Chapter 5

Be that as it may, to sum up the question of change, and the complication of all the factors and elements involved in its making is asking the impossible to know what did happen to bring all the difference of daily living in an earlier time to the customs of the present day. There is no solid proof or answer, and it has been this way from the beginning of time and God's creation of all things and the process of change will continue on as long as civilization stands.

Since change has brought so many good things for the benefit and improvement of man's living pattern as a whole, one may ask but what about those things that change has imposed on me that I hold little admiration for, if indeed any at all? And yet, the blessings of the improvements we enjoy and take comfort and contentment from allow us enough room in our beings to be able to tolerate those in society today who we dislike and do not adhere to and, sadly the list is long!

To be sure, there are many habits and customs in our society today that numerous citizens find wrong and unacceptable. To begin with, and the one change that takes priority over all the others, is moral behavior that falls into a number of categories. First on the list is young couples making a mockery of the instability of marriage by living together without God's holy sanction of the vows of marriage, not to mention that a great number of these couples bring children into this

The Death of the Neighborhood Church

world under this lawless circumstance. Another shocking behavior act, which of course, the Bible clearly condemns is same sex marriage.

Granted, the list is long that one is moved to take offense at, namely the lack of courtesy to our elders, insulting speech and contemptuous behavior in public, the blunt use of four-letter words that one hears and sees in print and far too often at that, and in particular a certain four-letter word that was doubtless ever uttered out loud in an earlier time, and if so, its meaning and the nature of it would have raised questions regarding it. Another offense is calling for and passing damnation on another person or mouthing words that may have ruffled or irritated some other person. Certainly, our yesterday society was a far cry from our present-day society.

Indeed, to point out how much some customs have changed, it has not been too long back in time when the movie actor Clark Gable said to Scarlett in "Gone with the Wind," "Frankly, my dear, I don't give a damn," the movie industry came near to censoring the phrase from the motion picture altogether! Then last and certainly not least by any means, is the level the politicians have fallen to. It appears and brings one to wonder if there is one exception among the majority of elected officials who are seeking reelection to the office they already hold as well as those of whom making an effort to gain the office they aspire to be elected to have not the first qualm about mouthing a lie to achieve their goal, which, of course, their constituents are fully aware of but give their support all the same, but such is the doings of politics! All in all, it does seem that with all the widespread decline in moral behavior, coupled with all the other shocking happenings, that little good is left in our society today compared to the modest customs of an earlier age. And yet, history tells us this was not the case at all. For these earlier times were filled with drawbacks and liabilities too. Though one is still urged to yearn for some of the ethical customs of this past age when so much was waiting for man to explore and experience. Still, and all too soon at that, our society was faced with another change and one that is rather difficult to understand and deal with, no matter how much effort one makes to do so.

Although the timing of its appearance is rather difficult to pinpoint, it seems the fad of free expression came to be the most popular notion or idea for one to adhere to or follow, and especially among the younger generation, shortly following World War II. Doubtless all the calamities – the distress and pain this four-year long war caused – induced some doctor of medicine and others in the sphere of medicine agreed that to be oneself, to give freely to one's emotions makes a far more well-balanced mind and healthy body, and restraining one's emotions is not the better way to handle most of the feelings that happen to assail us at times! Never mind the impact of freeing these emotions on others to endure, this fad of free expression is the most favored way to follow!

Therefore, few surprises are left to be discovered and experienced anymore, and apparently no line drawn against these unfavorable happenings, because it appears the greater number of people in our society today take the view that all this unbridled behavior is merely the freeing of one's emotions and should be of no over much concern to anybody!

Granted, the age in time that this writer grew up in, which included the years of "The Great Depression," was an age that was far from being without its liabilities as all societies in history have been. And yet, comparing the normal and accepted customs and habits of that day to all the astonishing rules of law and the accepted pattern of our society today, one is inclined to look back on these former yesteryears as certainly being a period of containing a lot of good and much innocence.

Assuredly, one thing among a great many other contrasts between this back in time day and the present day is the use of illicit drugs among the populace, which was unheard of and which nobody would have given any thought to if they had. For drugs were some kinds of medicine or treatment for some ailment that were found on the shelves of the local drug store, or the pharmacy department which required a doctor's prescription as a rule for something of a more serious nature. Certainly, there were no illicit, addictive and habit-forming drugs available such as heroin, cocaine or any other controlled drugs, and if anybody had desired any one kind of these illicit drugs it is safe to say they would not have had any success in obtaining them. But grievously, this is not the case in the present day. Because, for too long a time, these harmful drugs are peddled daily by some camouflage supplier to the unfortunate addict for money.

The one and only addictive substance that has been available to anyone who has a taste for it since time beginning, and is present in one form or another to some degree in numerous beverages as well as many kinds of medicine, is the intoxicating substance alcohol. And yet, despite its drawbacks and its remarkable factor of luring one's taste buds to not only relish its savoring sensations of transporting them to that illusory state of being on a higher plane than normal, and seeing and feeling that all is well with everything around them including the entire world and, at the same time having the power to stamp them as having become an alcoholic if they indulge too frequently, this all too common substance has served mankind in many helpful ways for long centuries.

Assuredly, alcohol has had a long important use and staying place in the field of medicine and has always been highly regarded as a disinfectant against infection-causing germs, and especially in the matter of raw wounds, surgical operations as well as any other cutting of body tissue. As a matter of fact, back in an earlier age when medical aid of any kind was most difficult to come by – oftentimes no doctor or medicine either – the first remedy or treatment that was thought of was to reach for the whiskey bottle or jug since whiskey is pretty much one hundred percent alcohol. That is, if the circumstances happened to be a gunshot wound where it was determined the bullet could be removed as well as all other open wound injuries and operations. And in spite of the terrible agony to the suffering victim, the whiskey was poured directly into the open wound, which, of course, made it necessary to restrain the victim as much as possible if they were still conscious, and the burden of that task fell upon the

The Death of the Neighborhood Church

person who was physically and emotionally geared as well to brave the ordeal without flagging out, too, and joining the unfortunate victim! In addition, if no pure whiskey was available to attempt to aid the victim, other spirits of some sort were substituted with some being more potent than the pure whiskey when it came to rendering the ill from the real world, the pain of the knife, distress of any sort or killing germs or anything else! The general concern was to deaden the victim's feelings above anything and all else! And, as incredible as it is, a great number of these unfortunates whom had very little going for them in these brutal situations did survive, no doubt, because of alcohol's effect on killing germs.

As a matter of fact, the majority of spirits were either "homemade," or distilled out in the wooded areas someplace at an apparatus built of different sorts that was referred to as a whiskey still. The two most common of these potent beverages were labelled "moonshine" and "white lightening," appropriately named to say the least! In any case, despite the crude apparatus and the remote wooded surroundings these two spirits were distilled in, the potent effect on one who drank either of the two, "moonshine" or "white lightening," was no less effective in depositing one on that high plane of delight that they desired to be than had they indulged in the most expensive whiskey ever distilled and marketed! Of course, distilling these two intoxicating substances or any other kind was in the period of time called Prohibition and was most assuredly against the law, which, to be sure, compelled the law to be pretty much occupied to be on the lookout for smoke billowing off in the woods someplace that, more often than not, was a sure sign of a whiskey still in operation.

However, in addition to it being unlawful to operate a whiskey still because of Prohibition, this period also was the time of the Great Depression when money was nearly extinct for a great number of people. Therefore, operating a whiskey still came to be a near common business for a great many people and a way to come by a little cash to have for their empty pockets. In truth, this period of time was a forbidding time for most people.

There were no jobs. Paid labor was almost impossible to come by. And if one were lucky enough to find a paying job, the average wage was a mere fifty cents a day with hours of labor stretching from sunrise to sunset, or even later, maybe continuing for twelve hours!

Thus, little wonder with such an appalling period for the majority of people that a great number of the labor class turned to making and selling intoxicating beverages in order to survive from hunger. Even those who lived more moderately were forced to watch every cent they spent including pocket change. That is, if they were lucky to have one cent in their pocket to start with. There was hardly one individual, no matter their station in life, who was spared the dire state of this depressing period and not affected by it to some degree. And, what was the state of affairs with the neighborhood church during this dreadful and forbidding time? Doubtless its minister as well as the deacons and leaders who occupied its Amen Corner on each and every Sunday morning, all looked the other way relative to one making whiskey by having a whiskey still off in the woods some place. In short, if the minister, deacons, leaders of the church or whoever were aware of a non-alcoholic person distilling spirits to sell in order to keep his family from starvation, the law would have had a far and wide hunt to locate his whiskey still! As a matter of fact, in this period of widespread hunger and reduced state of living conditions, a great number of church ministers gave freely of their position as the minister of the church they were assigned to and did not depend on their parishioners to furnish them much of anything relative to their own needs and daily living pattern. For they were more than aware that there would be very little put in the collection plate when it was passed around on Sunday morning regardless of how uplifting and interesting the sermon was. Therefore, most all ministers, in this time of burdens, were forced to see to his own livelihood because it would not be found in the collection plate when Sunday approached!

In fact, it was not uncommon for a man of the cloth, so to speak, to turn to farming. For the good earth was always there and a staying source to have a vegetable garden, growing grain for household use, and the farm animals, too, to say nothing of the horse or mule that pulled the plow to make the grain to start with as well as provide the transportation also to convey them to wherever there was a need to go to, because having the means to purchase an automobile was out of the question for not only the church minister, but the majority of people as well.

All in all, the Great Depression was a dire time for the majority of people and the neighborhood church was no exception from being affected, not only its spiritual leader but any and all people who entered its door to worship their God.

And yet, despite the trials and tribulations of this depressing time, the Great Depression, most all people without exception held and enjoyed a feeling of being privileged instead of feeling impoverished by an all-unseen prevailing spirit of closeness and concern for their fellow man, not only inside the neighborhood church on Sunday morning, but throughout the week with family members, one's neighbor, friends and acquaintances alike.

Still, the above is not to imply that everybody walked around in a state of bliss with no needs, no worries, or any down or low feeling at all, because, it is for sure, there was no one feeling that they were "in the clouds," either – so to speak. Indeed, there was plenty of worry and heartache too, an intense yearning for something better than what little there was at one's disposal, if not the missing item that was not there and would remain that way. But, even so, what did seem to be evident was a common state of acceptance of the circumstances of things in general and everybody adapting the best they could and making do with what they had to make do with and even sharing with others as much as their own means allowed them to. And, in addition to the seemingly general concern for another's welfare in this age in time, when some calamity did take place in the neighborhood, the unfortunate or a family as a whole was gifted in their needs by neighbors and friends banding together in a common cause to aid the person or family who had suffered the misfortune. In short, sympathy for others seemed to be far more in supply in those bygone days than it is nowadays, when one might come face-to-face with someone else who is obviously in low spirit by some kind of misfortune or calamity that has fallen upon them, about the most sympathy the misfortunate may come by or hear uttered by one's counterpart is the phrase, "I'm sorry," then and most likely and on the spot at that, the untroubled will continue on to wherever they were headed to, or do whatever they had in mind to do, nakedly freeing their thoughts from the oppressed and letting their mind concentrate on their own wants and doings.

No question, that when it comes to holding a great degree of interest and concern for someone else's problems or trouble – becoming involved, so to speak – there is a shift of near turnabout in our society today balanced to the way it was in a bygone day. In brief, an obvious naked lack of caring for the feelings of one's fellow man, prompting one to wonder and ask what happened to produce these far-out habits and behavior? In addition, and sadly and more alarming at that, is the heavy decline in the attendance of God's house of worship on Sunday morning. Of course, all these facts that do exist in our society in the present day and are startling to take in and give thought to, let us be aware that all those past yesteryears were not without their tragedies and calamities too.

The fact is, it appears as time moves on with one civilization falling after the one before it, that change is inevitable and each and every civilization and culture is different. And giving thought to this solid fact of ongoing change, one is persuaded to reason that perhaps the chief cause that prompts most people to go their own way and hold, seemingly, little regard for others is due more to the advancement that man has made through the ages than the makeup of man himself. Granted, with all the astounding material things at one's disposal today is a far cry from the raw existence of the cave man and the next generation following him who had no choice but live in closeness with their fellow man and depend on his support in order to survive the hardships of the living conditions. Hence, this way of thinking and looking at change is far more comfortable and pleasant to accept rather than mentally scorning our counterparts for their seemingly indifferent behavior in this present day.

Chapter 6

Speaking of tragedies and calamities moves my mind back to a tragedy that occurred in the neighborhood when I was a small child, but old enough to sense the seriousness and poignant feeling that seemed to fall over the entire community, marking it and all its residents with a seemingly deep loss and grief. And, although for all the good that alcohol has provided man for long ages in time, and especially as an agent in the medical field for keeping infectious germs at a minimum if not destroying them altogether, this intoxicating substance, alcohol, was the chief cause of the tragedy and resulted in two lives lost, a wife and the death of her husband one month later following her death.

It is not necessary to identify the victims of this tragedy, but it is morally fair and just to point out that they both were prominent and respectable residents of the community, and from all appearances and accounts were much devoted to one another. Though there were no children from the marriage, the lack of children appeared to affect their relationship none whatsoever. In short, from all visible signs the status of this couple's marriage would have been labeled a successful and loyal marriage. Although, there was an apparent troublesome and unfavorable drawback in regard to their union. The husband had a taste for alcohol and indulged in the substance rather often in one form or another. Still, despite the fact that he did fall into periods of indulging his desire for escaping from reality at times, one would not have labeled him a drunk, because he kept to his farming duties and the standard of his household living was equal to that of any of his neighbors. Further, he and his wife lived as independently and caring for themselves and each other and managing their own affairs no differently from any of their neighbors. If there was ever any offhand talk regarding this couple being unable to manage for themselves, it certainly was never open talk. Doubtless, what accounted for things going at a normal rate when the husband was on a binge of excessive drinking was his wife's capability to see that everything was kept in order until he did sober up.

At any rate, back in this age in time when few rural households could even boast to own a radio, and television was a marvel waiting in the future, not to mention that every household in the land would, eventually, come by one and doing away with the custom of neighbors visiting one another on a regular basis and enjoying one another's company as well as catching up on all recent happenings and news in the community. Still, with no warning or anything out of the ordinary going on relative with the couple in subject, imagine the shock and horror that swept the entire neighborhood as well as miles beyond it when the news spread that this man had shot and killed his wife while she was preparing their breakfast early one morning!

However, it had been vaguely talked and known about before the tragedy that his wife on occasion did hide his whiskey from him when she thought his binge had gone on long enough. Thus, sadly, this act on her part had sealed her fate with the first bottle of whiskey she had hidden. For the husband himself confessed he was aware that his wife did hide his whiskey from time to time. He confessed this to his half-brother, who happened to be the next-door neighbor to this writer's family. He told his half-brother that he awakened that morning and wanted a drink of whiskey in the worst way. He searched and searched for his whiskey bottle and, failing to find it and in his half-drunken, sodden brain, he approached his wife with his shotgun to tell him where she had hidden his whiskey and the gun fired accidently and killed her!

The county sheriff was informed. But not before the half-brother made certain the husband had become clearheaded and capable of telling what happened to the law authorities. At all events, the troubled and grieving husband must have been able and convincing enough with the telling of the tragedy. For he was not arraigned by the law authorities at that time, but was informed that he must answer to an indictment by law one month later, or within thirty days of the tragedy.

In the meantime, a number of close friends to the victim in the neighborhood went to the couple's residence to prepare the lady for burial. Then the victim's immediate family took charge of every detail regarding the burial of the remains, and the husband was not allowed to have his say in one thing regarding his wife's remains, her funeral, the cemetery where she was interred, her headstone and the wording on it – nothing! Throughout the entire affair, as well as for all time afterwards, it was as if she was never married to her husband or even known him. It is doubtful he was allowed to view his wife's remains even if he voiced his desire to see her. In fact, the tragedy was to result into a total one-sided event with the victim's family in charge of everything. In addition, if the living husband, his family members, friends to the victim or anyone else ever protested her family taking charge and overseeing all details to their satisfaction regarding her burial, it was never talked in the open and remained a closed subject. Today, it would be a different story altogether.

Granted, no matter the circumstances of a tragedy, or any happening of interest in this present-day society, both families connected by marriage would be very much involved and woe to any one person, including the law, who would attempt to instruct them to the contrary. To be sure, both families – maybe even a close friend to the victim – would be very much involved, and if all interested and concerned parties were unable to agree alike to all arrangements regarding the victim's burial, the end result would turn to the victim's remains being placed in a morgue until some solution between opposing parties could be worked out.

At all events, there is no question that the circumstances of most any happening that did fall in yesteryear, let it be a tragedy, an illness of unusual symptoms that no one was familiar with, or some other occurrence that was a surprise, was handled and carried through with in an entirely different way than in this present day. It brings one to wonder and ponder why, and ask was society as a whole more tolerant, broadminded and force-bearing in regard to their fellow man's feelings and his emotional state back then? In any case, it was certainly vastly different between then and now, and appears that the depth of misery was given more attention and concern by the majority of the populace in a past society.

Again, one may wonder and question the difference between the past and the present and ponder what did induce the apparent aloof attitude of this present day? Perhaps most of the cause lies in the quality of our society today. Whereas back in time man did not have the improvements and advancements in his living pattern that he has in this day and age, which, for the most part, makes for a far easier way of doing all the chores that are necessary in one's daily life. For back in an earlier age with so little basic improvements at man's disposal, and more often than not, he was confronted with a task that made it necessary to seek another person's help, which as a rule was usually his neighbor and which generated a closeness by association that otherwise would never have occurred had daily living been similar to the conditions of today. Therefore, it is more reasonable to view the aloofness and distance that is so obvious among the populace in our present society is not because man has changed so much in character and makeup, but because of all the improvements and advancements made as well as so many more things of interest to explore and experience that just simply were not there for him in an earlier time.

At any rate, the shocking and astounding news of

this neighbor woman's tragic death, to say nothing of the unusual circumstances of her burial, had hardly ceased to remain to be the subject that was talked throughout the neighborhood when its residents were suddenly rendered another terrible blow by the stunning news that the husband she had left had also departed from his earthly life!

No, he had not been shot by his own hand, nor by the hand of anyone else.

The word that was told and circulated throughout the community – and no other news connected with his death ever was to dispute or question this first report – was that the deceased had complained of a headache and taken an aspirin and gone to bed and in a short while was found dead! His death was nearly one month following that of his deceased wife, and a day or two before he was to appear and answer to the indictment regarding the tragic death and circumstances of her death.

After the death of his wife and her burial, the husband had lived with his half-brother and the latter's family who were the next door neighbors to this writer's own family and, that being the case, we were the first to hear the shocking report of his sudden death.

Although I was a child and young in years, I vividly recall the morning the astounding news of this man's death abruptly slicing through the air and hitting the neighborhood with no less impact than had a shot from a cannon been fired!

It happened to be that time of year when grading and tying the bright leaf cured tobacco into bundles was taking place, a chore that required most every family

The Death of the Neighborhood Church

member from children to grownup, sharecropper, tenant, as well as hired hands alike in order to get the tobacco ready for market before the local market closed and the tobacco warehouse buyers left to go to some other tobacco-growing states where a later and different kind of tobacco was grown and marketed.

On this particular morning and not long after everybody was settled down to the chore of grading the tobacco, that on this day was taking place at one of the four curing tobacco barns on the homeplace when, like a sudden clap of thunder, the next-door neighbor's son came running as fast as he was able to move his feet and blurted, in a shallow and barely audible breath "My uncle's dead!" Then, catching his breath somewhat and more in control of his emotions, he went on to disclose the headache and the aspirin and the finding of the corpse.

Immediately, my father rose from the chore he was engaged in and brushing a tobacco twig or a stray part of a tobacco leaf here and there from the clothes he was wearing, he joined the neighbor's son and set out for the duty that he was aware awaited him. This was the way, the patterns and the practice among neighbors and friends back then. The moment one became aware of some unusual happening such as a house on fire, a serious accident or sickness, and especially the news of someone's death, there was no hesitation about setting out for the site of the trouble. There was no thought of giving attention to any personal grooming. No thought of changing one's clothes to make a more suitable appearance. The only thing that mattered was to stop and put on hold whatever one was doing and set forth to the place of disturbance, or word of death, as quickly as one could make it to lend a hand of assistance in any capacity one was able to.

In the case of death, and in quite a number of cases, no mortician was called to prepare the remains for burial. All details for burial, or any other duty regarding the deceased's death, was done and carried out by close neighbors to the family, as well as the deceased. In the case of this man's sudden and unexpected death, my father and one or two other neighbor men prepared his remains for burial.

He was buried in a cemetery that contained a number of his family's relatives miles distant from the cemetery that contained his wife's grave! His burial was a solemn and quiet affair, hardly any display of emotion whatever. Though there was never any talk that his burial was any different from the usual way of most burials. And, most assuredly, there was no talk that his deceased wife lay in another cemetery. It seemed as though the tragedy that fell upon this couple was buried along with the last shovelful of dirt that filled his grave and that was the end of it, with everybody leaving the gravesite and going on about his or her own business! All the same, it prompts one to wonder and question whether all the moves and decisions that were made and carried through with by the relatives of this couple were wise and reasonable moves, laying them in their eternal sleep in different cemeteries? In that, who is to question that despite any and all opposition from her or his relatives, that their spirits did not unite with the other and ultimately rest someplace together for all eternity in spite of every move made regarding the tragedy?

Of course, because of this man's sudden death, there was no meeting with law authorities, no indictment or legal action ever taken regarding his or his wife's death. His burial was the finality of all the tragic happening and the last of it.

Further, and without question, the tragedy that befell this couple would never have occurred but for the weakness of one indulging in any kind of alcoholic beverage to the excess.

Chapter 7

Time does have a way of marching on, and the happenings of the past whether they are tragic, joyful, or otherwise are all events that are past and gone and only can be revived again and brought back to us as a memory in our minds – to recall and in a sense lived again. And what a blessing to be able to recall some happy experience that gave us a deep and abiding joy and filled our hearts with eager expectation – a past memory of joy and delight that affects our being no less than had we taken some soothing tonic. And, no question, it is a given and only normal that we tend to recall those happenings and events that gave us the most joy and delight and push those that brought us deep pain and grief from our minds as often as possible is truly a godsend and blessing too. For to bury ourselves in the grief and agony of losing a much-loved one, or allow some mournful incident to overwhelm our state of well-being and doubtless cast us into a deep depression besides, would certainly take away all expectation within us to enjoy all aspects of the beauty as well as the gifts that life holds for us.

So, the better and most healthful way is to strive to make the effort to keep our minds and our hearts open to optimism and expectation as much as we possibly can and look forward to meeting what the next day may hold, because the wonder of another day and then the expectations we may meet is the beauty and joy of

The Death of the Neighborhood Church

another tomorrow.

Once again, and going back in time and how things were in general in this past period, this writer's thoughts not only return to that small, white-painted church that sat off from the neighborhood crossroads – its steeple a staying symbol of hope and expectation, symbolizing the prospect of seeing and being with friends on Sunday morning – but also instilling a sense of joy in looking forward to singing those long-ago hymns that seemed to lift one's very soul into the entity of God's holy kingdom was the crowning of all expectation.

Sadly, however, most all later modern ministers turn away from those old spirituals that were sung with such joy in favor of some other hymn that they feel is more in accord with the sermon they have selected to deliver for that Sunday's worship service. If indeed the minister did refer to some Bible text at all in preparing his or her sermon, because most sermons are so lukewarm and unmoving, it is doubtful any biblical text was involved whatever but merely the minister's conception and belief of his or her subject! Further, regarding the hymn chosen for the worship service, which the minister views is more fitting for his sermon, more often than not the congregation is at a total loss to even hum along with the unfamiliar wording and musical notes, let alone make any attempt to lift voice to it! Therefore, considering these two very important aspects of a worship service nowadays, the chosen hymns and the unmoving, lukewarm sermons, one does not have to wonder and question the true reason for the greater part of the decline in attendance of the majority of churches today.

Actually, in truth, like most everything else in the walk of life and the course of steps man takes and follows in this present day, there is hardly any comparison between a worship service in those long-ago days and the usual worship service of today. For example, most sermons that are delivered from the pulpit nowadays are nearly void of any enthusiastic verbal expressions in regard to the biblical teachings of Christ whatsoever! The average sermons that are spoken from the pulpit today border merely above the impact of average talk with maybe some reference to a biblical incident thrown in now and then, and to be sure, he or she will not be giving voice to their message overlong at that!

Nothing more, nothing less for the worship sermon!

Certainly, the above assertion is taking a somewhat harsh stand relative to the majority of ministers of the church today. But, even so, there will hardly be one person who will protest this assertion, or disagree with it, if the subject does happen to come up. Thus, obviously, the fault for the decline in the attendance and less interest in the church, as a whole, lies more with the assigned minister to the neighborhood church due to his or her shortcoming to meet the ability level their profession calls for rather than the members of the church who they are supposed to serve as well as give religious counsel to if necessary. Therefore, all ministers should readily acknowledge the lack of skill on their part and shoulder some of the obvious decline in his or her assigned church and make an all-out effort to recognize the problem and improve it as much as possible, which, of course, doubtlessly could be brought to fruition by some degree anyway, if there were more inspiring sermons to hear and a revival of the old joyful hymns to sing, instead of some hymn the attending members of the church are totally unfamiliar with.

However, a minister's ability to inspire his listeners or the singing of the hymns are not the only factors involved in the decline of church attendance today. There is much more at stake to deal with and a much more serious problem at that, and one that, regretfully, is boldly displayed in all walks of society and that is moral behavior in this present day!

Granted, the years before and during the years of World War II and a number of years following the conflict of said war, the majority of our society as a whole held to the concept of accepted moral behavior and practiced its principles and standard of ethics in one's daily life with no thought of behaving otherwise. Then as astonishing as it is, and one would be hard put to establish when and what happened, it suddenly appears that no matter how outlandish the situation or one's behavior that hardly anyone is offended or disturbed to one degree and merely accepts it as a matter of fact – no more, no less! Moreover, it also appears that if the greater number of law officials, or those who are in authority, are offended by this obnoxious behavior when it does occur that pretty much to the extent of their reaction is to merely turn their heads in another direction and go on about their own business rather than making public that they are offended and begin to make some effort to mend the situation if possible.

And yet, on the other hand, in this present day, there is always the question of what the consequences might turn into if one is moved to become involved with some unruly individual or disruptive group of people. And, make no mistake, any one person has just reason to view these unfavorable situations with a reluctant attitude even though it is deeply disappointing and discouraging to the majority of society.

In the society of yesteryear, the law did exercise its authority to the fullest and carried out its duty as well without giving one thought to the possibility of having to face a judge and jury in a court of law for doing the job they pledged under oath to do in the service of their state, county and community. But, in this day and age, the rule of law has become so complicated that any aspect of exercising any part of it is a horse of another color, so to speak!

Therefore, it appears that no matter the event, or public gathering of any sort or how important or whatever, these disruptive groups of people, protesters or whatever complaint some of them may have to scream and holler about will show up. It does not make one iota bit of difference to them that others have come to hear or gain more information regarding the subject of interest of the event. All that matters to those offenders is that their voices or their wants might triumph over the event whether they obtain any worth from it or not. Of course, in years past, if there were any disturbances by any one person, or group of people at a public event, a church gathering, a private residence, or any place else, those offenders responsible were taken into custody and forced to bend to the law. Hence, one may ask or question what happened to bring all this discord and unrest in today's society? Who is responsible for all this harmful and injurious change? Whose hand is accountable and at whose feet does the blame lie when an officer of the law is limited from carrying out his duty for fear of what his action might result into?

In truth, and the fact is, no one person is truly accountable for all this underlying change that is liable to hurl its ugly existence at any public event at any given moment simply because of the fad of free expression, a trend or craze that has originated among the young, and doubtless, too, because of their boredom for lack of being involved in some project of interest that would occupy their mind and induce them as well as giving them a sense of doing something worthy.

In short, another factor that has come to have a great influence on this obvious lack of interest for some worthy cause relative to a great number of the young is, most often they have come to be a recipient of having too much too soon in regard to material things to explore and enjoy! Then again, let us not rule out that this craze of protesting might have taken root and made a lasting impact on the young and added fuel to the idea of protesting, because of the movie actress, Jane Fonda, going to Vietnam and protesting the war in North Vietnam in spite of thousands upon thousands of United States servicemen in South Vietnam serving in this war by having been drafted there.

Apparently, it did not make one iota of difference to Jane Fonda that by publicly displaying her own opinions and dislike for war in North Vietnam, that she had little regard, if any at all, for not one United States soldier, South Vietnam, or anything else but herself. From all accounts, her protesting this conflict in person by riding upon an armored tank in North Vietnam meant no more to her than performing in another movie! Her presence there was a dishonor to all soldiers and especially those unfortunate ones who lost their lives there.

In truth, no one person is in favor of any nation turning to war to settle its disputes and disagreements with some other nation. But, even so, in so many cases, war is inevitable because of the circumstances involved. For instance, World War II is an example. For our sitting President, Franklin D. Roosevelt, was given no choice but to ask Congress to declare a state of war against the nation of Japan and its allies when Japan staged its sneak attack at Pearl Harbor on December 7, 1941, and nearly destroyed the entire United States Naval fleet anchored in its harbor, not to mention the three thousand or more lives lost.

In addition, if there was ever any one person who was inclined to protest this four-year war with the nation of Japan, as well as Nazi Germany, they most certainly kept it under wraps, so to speak. For this war was a universal cause, every United States citizen's fight to defend and save this country from hostile aggression, including everybody, no matter their station in life. Not one household escaped from being affected and made a sacrifice in some way, with a great number of households paying the ultimate sacrifice by losing a loved one in the fighting forces. Indeed, this

The Death of the Neighborhood Church

was a war that united all American citizens together with each and all showing and projecting their love and loyalty and their willingness to do anything they could do to defend America against the enemy.

No, there were no groups of people – protesters – marching and screaming and carrying signs with offensive wording. This type of movement emerged into our society in the years of post-World War II. And, if the birth of protesting was not born in this period of time when Jane Fonda, the actress went to North Vietnam and protested America giving its support to South Vietnam because of North Vietnam's aggression of the latter, no doubt her action regarding this conflict between these two foreign countries gave a great deal of momentum to the protesting movement!

At any rate, no matter when this movement was born. nor when or where or who is responsible for it appearing in our society, from all accounts it certainly appears it is here to stay. For it seems that there is no end to a group of people protesting some law or subject matter at any given time nowadays. And, not only protesters marching and carrying signs indicating their grievances in an orderly fashion, but as disturbing and astonishing as it is, a number of these protesters burning and destroying any property that happens to be in their path along with foul language as well as violence against anyone who happens to disagree with them, the law included, which is most astounding to witness in a civilized and, supposedly, cultured society.

All the same, and as alarming and anxious as it is to see, protesting some grievance has become so common and popular that it is not a surprise at all to see young teenagers caught up in the excitement of a group of protesters and marching along with them, and worse still, there is no doubt the majority of these youngsters haven't got the least idea or understanding why the event is taking place in the first place! Most of them are there because it is just something different to do – something far more interesting and exciting than the normal run of a day's activities, which, of course, is not doing much if anything aside from some mundane usual chore. To be sure, a far cry from what circumstances were in a bygone time when everyone in an average household from grownup to the teenager had little time to spare because of the numerous chores required to maintain and keep everything going toward having a successful annual yearly income, and especially when so much labor was done by hand because the many improvements were to come in later years such as the automotive tractor and other mechanical devices in point of operating a farm.

In short, relative to growing up on a farm in earlier years, and especially in the bright leaf tobacco season, there was no time for anybody to become restless for lack of something to do!

Indeed, it was work and work aplenty every day of the week aside from Sunday.

And, it goes without saying, Sunday was the day that was held in anticipation by each and all who grew up on a tobacco farm as this writer did, a day in the week that restored one's faith in the knowledge of God's love for us as well as that all earthly things are connected with Him and His heavenly kingdom.

Yes, in this bygone era, one left the neighborhood

church on Sunday harboring a feeling of spiritual awakening and closeness with God, along with their heart filled with a blessedness by the wording of those old, beloved hymns that were sung during each and every worship service and inducing a deep and abiding faith also of an anticipation within one's being to meet the next Sunday's worship service for a certainty.

Chapter 8

Time, no two ways about it, does not stand still. It continues to move on, counting the days, the weeks, the months and the years over and over and in the same cycle with no end. And, not only does it bring us the four different seasons that fall with a mark of difference from the one before it and making up an entire year, but we come to recognize that the pattern of our daily living, the custom of how we might have gone about doing some daily task, a relationship with others, some fellowship we enjoyed and counted on, not to mention the unexpected loss and grief of a loved one – all of it brings to mind that no one thing stays the same and holds to the normal without undergoing some change as time moves on and is a solid and true fact of life and one's existence here.

And so, with the years falling one after another with little variation from the one before it, aside from these inevitable changes that do fall in any given year and at any time, before any one person had given a thought to the possibility of it happening and in no way could have been prepared for it not one degree, World War II erupted like a sudden thunder clap over the entire world and bringing with it the greatest surprise and shocking change that was possible for anyone to imagine.

Granted, those Japanese planes bombing Pearl Harbor, Hawaii, on December 7, 1941, in a sneak attack, not only opened World War II – a worldwide war that was to continue for four long years – but brought changes that nobody had experienced before like food stamps and many material items that were manufactured on a much lower scale, because supporting our armed forces with material goods, as well as the necessary equipment to fight the enemy, took priority over everything else. And yet, all the effort, endurance of doing without material things, the sacrifice and grief of losing a loved one in the fighting forces, it is safe to say that comparing how things were in general – habits, customs, morals, and the daily living pattern during the war years – to the changes that were to come in a mere few years following the war years is enough to bring one to gasp in wonder and surprise! For the age in time, as well as the years during this worldwide conflict, deserves to be labeled a time of quiet and innocence compared to the unheard of and shocking changes that were to emerge into society a short while later. Even the neighborhood church was not spared from undergoing these inevitable changes. For, gradually, it became apparent that all the things the church had ever signified and gave meaning to and was symbolic with – its staying power and *?* spirit, the old moving hymns, the inspiring sermons and social gatherings – were slowly disappearing and being replaced by mostly short and unmoving worship sermons, hymns that, as a rule, the choir was only familiar with because of having practiced the musical sound and lyrics of the hymn, to say nothing of the various social events that were held at the church such as the exciting and happily awaited event called a box supper, in which attractively wrapped boxes of savory food were auctioned to the highest bidder with the owner's name inside the box, and which the bidder never knew who they would have the pleasure of eating supper with until opening the box. This event called for a lot of joy and surprise, too. And, no doubt, a few letdowns as well.

At any rate, and all too soon at that, the box suppers were no more as well as other social get-togethers, habits and customs connected with the neighborhood church with other changes relative to its worship service becoming the pattern to follow and adhere to. And granted and more in point and certainly not excluded in all these changes taking place is the minister's sermon, which is the main point of the worship service and which has become so short and lukewarm, not to mention unmoving, that it leaves the churchgoer yearning for so much more, yearning to feel something more emotionally relative to God and His teachings from the way they felt before they entered the church in the first place!

But, more often than not, and unfortunately at that, the spiritual uplifting that the churchgoer is yearning and seeking is not to be gained by attending most churches in this present day. For instead of leaving a worship service feeling uplifted and with a spiritual closeness with God, it is most likely the average churchgoer's mind has become crowded by all those circulars that were inserted inside the service program that day – numerous notices and dates of events scheduled for the week ahead – the finance and board directors meeting along with numerous other notices asking for a donation to some charity organization, or aid to a foreign state or country one is hard put to recall if they have ever heard of it, not to mention other types of fliers asking for funds. In addition, and above all these financial burdens and obligations, remains the largest financial burden of all – the presiding minister's salary, which is an outlay in pay that has become a ridiculous amount in the present day, and especially, considering the personal attention most ministers render to the parishioners of the church, to say nothing of the little real amount of labor they do regarding the position they hold!

So, little wonder the great number of men, and women too, who have come to feel that they are God-called to preach the gospel in this age in time! For choosing to become a minister of the church has become a most rewarding occupation to follow nowadays! Because, pray tell me, what other vocation could one choose that most every cent and responsibility that is required of one to meet their daily living and livelihood cost is paid by other means besides their own funds! To be sure, the ministers of today who serve most churches regardless of the denomination of the church are well rewarded for their service. To be more forthright on the subject, ministers mainly only have the responsibility of buying their own food and clothing for themselves and family members. The balance or most of the rest of their living expenses is met by the church they are assigned to serve. They are furnished a residence to live in rent-free. All utilities are furnished. Their health insurance and travel expense is paid by the church, or any place else of interest they want to explore as well as all other expenses, minor or otherwise related to the church they serve.

Thus, considering all the above benefits that ministers of the church come by in the present day, it does not require an awful lot of mental work to see and understand why the study of theology has become so interesting and appealing to a great many men and women upon entering a higher institution of education and learning! Indeed, whether any man or woman is equipped with qualities of character, or induced by a deep faith and belief in God and His Word to truly desire to serve Him by becoming a minister of the church, the question only lies with him or her to answer! For it is obvious that a great number of church ministers fall way short of being capable of delivering an adequate and moving sermon from the pulpit, much less a praiseworthy one to God! More to the point, however, a minister who preaches the gospel should possess the talent to deliver the word of God in a manner that spiritually reaches his or her listeners and moves them to desire a closer relationship with God as well as persuade them to publicly project this want and need by attending worship services on a regular basis.

Be that as it may, though, the above statements and observations are indeed the circumstances and conditions of the church in the present day. And in reflection and sadly at that and certainly the most downcast change relative to the religious movement goes back to that small frame neighborhood church that sat off from the community crossroads so long ago. Not only is the framework that held every board and joist in it together long torn down and nothing left but vacant

The Death of the Neighborhood Church

ground where it sat, but its ***walfing?*** spirit that engulfed each and every person who entered its doorway has no doubt been lost someplace in the journey of building a new brick church in a different location – the spirit of the old church fading away and undergoing a near death in the new church's invading spirit, which is lacking somewhat in reaching the level of the overall uplifting that one came by in that old church of yesteryear. Still, thankfully, its name, Bethel Church, was preserved and honored by the new church keeping it for its own.

All the same, regarding all the change in the habits and customs the church has undergone and remains to be changing rapidly from what it once was – actually, as if it has been stricken with a declining sickness – not to mention the shrinking number of people who seek it out for spiritual guidance and have a closer relationship with God, our entire society as a whole has become deeply affected as well with all the change that has and is taking place nonstop it seems. As a matter of fact, with all the change in our present-day society, it might deserve to come by having certain names as likewise to other periods in history. For instance, the period in time that is labeled the age of Darwinism. Though whether his theory concerning the origin of life was or ever believed by any one person is questionable. Another period in time that came by a name was known as the Dark Ages when the population of all the continent of Europe was nearly wiped out by the dread bubonic plague – a bacterium affliction that millions upon millions of people succumbed to or were deeply affected by it. Then came the Victorian Age. The presumably virtuous period during the long reign of

Queen Victoria of England. This period in time could very well have been labelled the Chaste Age. For it is reported the queen was ever of virtuous conduct and any type of intimate behavior that even hinted at physical desire, let alone sexual, was simply taboo during the time she sat on the throne. There was no public kissing. No close hugging or touching. About the limit of acceptable behavior in public between man and woman, the latter was allowed to extend her gloved hand for the man to plant his kiss upon, if he so wished to do, which did possibly display they might be attracted to one another! And yet, it is most astonishing that all these chaste rules of conduct took root and became the normal and expected way of society during Victoria's reign, considering that this queen, herself, eventually came to hold the honorable distinction of supplying most every throne in Europe with one of her and her Consort Albert's numerous offspring! Which, of course, is sound fact that, despite all chaste rules of behavior that Victoria was noted for, she had no qualms about doing what she desired to do in the privacy of her bedroom with Albert!

Regarding these periods in history that did come to be named in a certain manner, and considering the changes that have brought our own society to its present-day footing, it has become apparent that the majority of society would not disagree that the custom of our living pattern is rapidly becoming a self-interest style of living and going our own way with hardly any concern for our fellow man or anything else aside from our own doings, which of course, is the making of a singular society and could rightly become to be called an age of Individualism! For there are few people in our society today who would disagree that the majority of the populace are inclined to be wrapped in the interest of their own private sphere of existence they have built for themselves and appear to be happy to dwell in and, at the same time, let the outer world pass by without taking one iota of notice to it!

Granted, from all appearances and, as sad as it is, the above analysis is the circumstance and state of our society today. And, moreover, it appears there will be no end to all the changes we are becoming exposed to and becoming acquainted with and, to be sure, some we certainly could live without! One example, and doubtless at that, there are a great number of lawmakers today who hold an official position to which they have been elected to as well as trusted to serve the people in their designated district, state, and country who fall way short in doing justice to the office they hold simply because their main interest in life is gaining something for themselves.

To be sure, instead of the majority of lawmakers focusing their minds and time on some worthwhile idea or devising some law that would benefit all citizens and seeing that it was voted on and passed into law, a great number do nothing but merely grace their office with their presence even when some tragedy or unexpected trouble or calamity falls. Then, rather than going to the scene of the tragedy or unexpected event in person to express their sympathy and see that assistance is given to those who are in need and suffering for material loss, not to mention the loss of a loved one due to the tragedy, some officials center their attention on some insignificant symbol or maybe a flag or monument that has been standing well over hundreds of years in honor of some historical figure and suggest or order it to be removed! Doubtless, this type of action by any law official has nothing to do with any kind of trouble that occurs, but only to improve their political standing with certain groups of the populace to obtain their vote certainly, removing some symbol of past history or any monument in honor of some person will never solve or remedy to any degree any tragedy or trouble that has happened, or ever restore the loss of a life, or correct the problem that caused the tragedy to happen in the first place.

Yes, instead of putting some inborn talent to use that perhaps they are not even aware they possess in making an effort to solve an unexpected problem or some trouble that takes place and try to find a solution that might help or make an impact and change some aspects of the problem for the better, or maybe do away with it altogether, the majority of lawmakers do nothing or merely offer some change that will have no benefit whatever on society as a whole. Granted, and it is a rare case when some elected official will devise some law and a law that is original within itself for the benefit and welfare of the people as a whole nowadays. For it is obvious that the majority who hold an office and have the power to make a difference only make everything as easy as possible for themselves, and certainly something that will benefit their own pocket, if they are inclined to do anything at all! And, worse still, a number of law officials will fall back on history, or some historical happening that occurred so long back

The Death of the Neighborhood Church

in time that the greater number of the populace are unable to recall if they have ever read or heard about it when not one single thing relative regarding the past event will help in solving the current problem at hand. Because history is history. It cannot be revived or changed and belongs in the sphere of its making and no place else. It cannot be undone, or altered to something other than the happening or circumstance that made it become history in the first place.

At all events, all law officials have an obligation to keep in mind that they were not elected to the office they came by and hold by only one group of citizens in their district, state, or country. They were elected by society as a whole, not just one ethnic group of people or race of citizens, but by a mixed culture of people who hold different views and beliefs and ideals that belong only to them and no one else. Further, these same citizens cast their vote on behalf of these lawmakers because they trusted the latter would serve and support them in a just cause.

Therefore, by removing any historical symbol from a building, a flag from a flagpole that is symbolic of a past event and flying in honor of the thousands of soldiers who fought in defense of it, not to mention the great number of lives lost, as well as ordering monuments displaying some historical person torn down, all of this type of action no elected official should engage in. For to do so is publicly attempting to appease one group of people for their view and belief and scorning another race or group for theirs, which is a move that is racist. Nothing more. Nothing less. So, it is far wiser to let the past remain as history, which it is and stop at trying to revise it into something it never was to start with.

The one and only sensible way that one can regard history is to think and look upon it and view it in the perspective, which, of course, is to consider any and all elements involved that generated it into the classification of being history, and if its making brought any benefit or good to the nation itself as well as mankind, be thankful and grateful to have the opportunity to honor it in this respect and do so. On the other hand, if some part of this same history is unacceptable to other citizens who have no desire to recognize it, much less honor and respect it in remembrance of its happening, we can try and should be more understanding and tolerant of their view with as much dignity as possible, and let the matter go and put it in the past where it belongs. For regardless of any one person's view or feelings, it is history and will remain history and more importantly, we live in the present and not in past events, come what may! In addition, history is likewise to the fact of change. Both will come to fall in its own designated time as time comes and falls with no end and will be thus for all eternity.

And, going back to the subject of change, what more proof could we come by to acknowledge that it is inevitable taking into account the recent news concerning the twenty-dollar bill of money! Yes, despite the fact this bill of money has been in circulation for a century or more, some lawmaker – who is probably incapable of using his or her mind to focus on something that might be of some benefit or something worthwhile to the populace they were elected to serve – has come up with the outlandish idea of changing the face of this bill of money to another image who the majority of people have never heard of or knew she even existed! Pray tell me, if anybody can, what impact or good will any one person come by in this present day by changing this bill of money to another image? Will it cause one to feel one bit different to have the privilege of spending twenty dollars or be more thrilled that it will cover some item we sorely want? That is, if we're lucky enough to have twenty dollars to spend in the first place? I think not!

All in all, however, history will continue to be a part of our lives and continue to be a question of better or worse at that.

And, last but by no means least, that small frame neighborhood church that set off at the junction of the community crossroads fell victim to this inevitable change and is no more. But, even so, the hope, expectation, and the spirit that its presence ever symbolized and induced each and every person who entered its door is a blessing to recall in remembrance. But sadly, this is not the state of most churches in this present day with the majority of them in decline.

Still, we must hold to faith and trust and try to go forward and embrace each and every day with hope, expectation, and enthusiasm.

It is the better way.

Made in United States
Orlando, FL
17 July 2024